NATHANAEL-ISRAEL ISRAEL, PhD

Origin of the Spiritual World

OTHER BOOKS BY NATHANAEL-ISRAEL ISRAEL

Get them at your local bookstore, or online (e.g. on Amazon, Science180.com/books)

Turbulent Origin of the Universe
There is Only One Scientific, Simple, Safe, Trustworthy, Unexpensive, Brave, Practical, Nonconformist, Universal, Verifiable Formula that Accurately Decodes the Universe Formation ... But You Are Not Using It

Reconciling Science and Creation Accurately
What Science Accurately Teaches about Creation and God's Existence that Atheists, Freethinkers, and even Most Christians Don't Know ... And How to Demonstrate it Without Falling into the Trap of Taking Sides Between Rationality and Faith

Turbulent Origin of Chemical Particles
Why You Don't Have to Embrace Evolution, Big Bang, or Deny God to Scientifically Prove the Formation of All Chemical Particles

From Science to Bible's Conclusions
How Decoding the Universe-Origin by Properly Revisiting Scientific Data—That Top Scientists Collected but Wrongly Analyzed—Bizarrely led to the 3500 Years Old Biblical Account of Creation

Turbulent Origin of Life
Why You Don't Have to Embrace Evolutionism or Check Your Brain at the Door in the Name of Faith or Science to Accurately Decrypt the Origin of Life Using the Historic Formula of the Universe Formation

How God Created Baby Universe
What Children Need to Scientifically Learn Early about the Universe Formation to Avoid Dangerously Abandoning God Later in Life Just Like Most College Students Who Embrace Evolutionism, Big Bang, and other Theories That Deny Biblical Creation

How Baby Universe Was Born
How to Scientifically Talk to Children about the Universe Formation and They will Know Forever How to Correctly Test the Intersection of Science and Faith

Science180 Accurate Scientific Proof of God
Can We Scientifically Explain the Formation of the Universe Through Natural Processes Without Evoking Evolution and Big Bang?

More books written by Nathanael-Israel Israel can be found at Israel120.com/books

NATHANAEL-ISRAEL ISRAEL, PhD
Founder of Science180: www.Science180.com
Father of Science180 Creationism

Origin of the Spiritual World

Top Secrets about the Origin of Everything in the Universe that Some Elites Have Hidden from You for Thousands of Years

Science180
Augusta, Georgia
United States of America
www.Science180Publishing.com

Copyright © 2025 by Nathanael-Israel Israel
Visit the author's website at Israel120.com

Origin of the Spiritual World
Top Secrets about the Origin of Everything in the Universe that Some Elites Have Hidden from You for Thousands of Years

First edition: October 2025

Published by Science180
Augusta, Georgia (USA)
www.Science180Publishing.com

Book Cover and Illustrations by Nathanael-Israel Israel

ISBN: 979-8-9932150-4-4

Library of Congress Control Number: 2025921112

All rights reserved. For permission requests, please visit Science180.com/permissions. Thank you for your support of the author's rights.

Neither the publisher nor the author shall be liable for any loss of profit or any other damages, including but not limited to special, incidental, consequential, personal, commercial, or other damages. More about copyright and disclaimers at Science180.com/copyright

More books by the same author can be found at Israel120.com and Science180.com

For information about special discounts available for bulk purchases, please visit Science180.com/discount for more details.

Science180 can bring authors including Dr. Nathanael-Israel Israel to your live or recorded events. For more information or to book an event, please visit Science180.com/speaking

For any questions, please visit Science180.com/contact

To publish your book(s) with Science180 Publishing, go to Science180Publishing.com

To interview the author of this book, visit Israel120.com/interview
To donate, please visit Israel120.com/donate or Science180.com/donate.

Printed in the United States of America.

CONTENT

Disclaimers...6

1. How I discovered Deep spiritual secrets that people have hidden for millennia—Were they CONCEALED because they WEre warring against the Bible or science?1

2. Shocking secrets that Enoch, the man who walked with God, saw on his journey from the Earth to the extremities of the whole universe ... (and how they can benefit you) 11

3. Miss this unconventional story about the formation of the spiritual and physical world and you will never know the key to open the scientific and Biblical gate that cracked the universe-origin...28

4. Why do people ignore this indisputable story about the formation of angels and their control of celestial bodies—yet their life depends on it even if they don't know? 45

5. Discover the indescribable secret life (unmentioned in the Bible) of the first human beings and how you can learn from it to improve your life today................63

6. Did the fall of the prince of this world cause the Earth to lose anything and become a terrible place where evil forces dominate?..68

7. What is life on Earth supposed to be and why do human beings suffer today? Did we or the Earth lose anything we cannot recover?..77

8. Why and how did some angels delight in corrupting the Earth knowing that they would eventually pay a huge price—or didn't they foreknow what is awaiting them? 94

9. How the first human beings were bailed out of their gigantic mistake that would have totally disconnected them from the uttermost joy forever (and how you too can avoid crashing your life)...101

10. Unearth the amazing story behind the formation of time, eternity, and end of the universe (and what you can do to live happily forever) 109

11. Seven secrets you ignore about the journey of Enoch to heaven and what he did when God commanded him to publish heavenly secrets for the benefit of human beings...119

12. The secrets about the origin of the universe, life, and angels hidden in the rejected books—that you won't learn at most churches—because THEY don't want you to know or they don't know them 128

NEXT STEPS OF THE JOURNEY 135

REFERENCES 143

INDEX..145

ABOUT THE AUTHOR...150

DISCLAIMERS

Called the pseudepigraphic version of my book on the origin of the universe, this book is an extended version of *"Reconciling Science and Creation Accurately"*, the Biblical version of my book on the origin of the universe. If you did not read that book yet, I encourage you to do so, for it will help you to better understand certain mysteries revealed in this book. In fact, most of the things I mentioned in this book were supposed to be in the aforementioned Biblical version. But as I was writing that book, I noticed that some ill-informed people who may be reading it may not understand its content or may be confused because it contains pseudepigraphic scriptures, which some people still consider as uninspired, yet they were inspired. Therefore to make my message consistent with the Biblical audience, I decided to write this book for those who want to know more about the pseudepigraphic story of creation. Above all, it is important that the readers of my writing understand that one of my goals is to NEVER go against God and His message in the Bible. No one should ever consider my interpretations of the Bible and the scientific data available as of the date of the publication of my books as something above the universal Word of God. The word of God revealed in the Bible, and which perfectly agrees with the Books of Enoch are authoritative. Though people may have made mistakes in translating the content of some materials, readers should be careful and prayerful not to misjudge something revealed by God.

My prayer is that, before I leave this world for heaven, I impact many lives, positively revolutionize science, impart true knowledge on people, strengthen the faith of the believers, and help many unbelievers come to Jesus to be saved. Though I believe God revealed certain things to me, it is also probable that, as a writing by a human, my books may contain interpretation mistakes, which may be found and addressed later as more revelations will be known and more scientific discoveries will be made. Therefore, no one should ever consider my commentaries of the scriptures as absolute and/or free from errors. I did my best to transmit what I think is the best explanation of scientific data and revelations known as of 2025. Should any error still exist in this book and the others I wrote, I ask God to forgive me, and help me and/or my readers to detect and fix them for His glory. For to God alone must be the honor, glory, and the praise for creating such a perfect world and giving us the grace to live in it and prepare ourselves for eternity. I also pray that this book helps you in your journey to heaven. When we will get there, we may finally know everything if God wants. Until I have a chance to talk about these mysteries with you again, be careful and prayerful about what you think you know. May the knowledge of the glory of God fill the earth as the waters cover the sea.

CHAPTER 1: INTRODUCTION

CHAPTER 1

HOW I DISCOVERED DEEP SPIRITUAL SECRETS THAT PEOPLE HAVE HIDDEN FOR MILLENNIA—WERE THEY CONCEALED BECAUSE THEY WERE WARRING AGAINST THE BIBLE OR SCIENCE?

1.1. Is the spiritual world real?
- What is the spiritual world?
- Where does it come from?
- What are its characteristics?
- How are the elements of the spiritual world organized?
- Do we interact with them on a daily basis or do they live far away?
- Why are most people not aware of the spiritual world–or are they?
- Where do our thoughts, ideas, imaginations, and intuitions come from?
- Are our emotions controlled by spirits?
- What are spirits and how were they formed?
- How can people communicate with spirits—or do most people already do that but ignore?
- What is the origin of angels and what is their job?
- Who created Satan and the demons?
- Why are there so many problems in this world?
- Are we the only beings in the universe–if not, how can we know and interact with the other beings beyond the Earth?

ORIGIN OF THE SPIRITUAL WORLD

- Is there really a life after death and if so, how can we know it?
- Was the spiritual world formed before the physical world that we see?
- What are the interactions between the spiritual world and the physical world, and can you profit from them?
- Can your doubts about spiritual things make the spiritual world unreal?
- If God did not create Himself, how did He come into existence?
- Did God tell us How He created the universe, but we ignored it?
- Where was God before creation?
- Who created God or how did He create Himself?
- What was life like for the first human beings on Earth?
- Why did they fail and what can we learn from their experiences?
- Can we see spiritual beings with our physical eyes–if not, why not?

Indeed, most people in this world only know or focus their attention on the physical world that surrounds us: the planets, the asteroids, the moons, the comets, the meteoroids, the stars, and the galaxies in the sky in one hand, and in the other hand, the human beings, the plants, the animals, the insects, the bacteria, the fungi, the viruses (such as Covid-19 that troubled the world in 2019) and some of the other touchable living things they deal with every day. But is all that exists really limited to those physical things only?

After spending about half a century on this planet called Earth, and going through various things both in Africa and in America, I can indisputably report that, there is more in this world than what we can physically see. From the ghosts or demons to God the Creator (in whom I believe), passing by the holy angels that some people believe in, while others deny, the physical world is filled with and controlled by "invisible" beings and forces that most people ignore, yet they interact with them every day. However, some people are well aware of the existence and functioning of the spiritual world, the world of spirits.

I would not have understood some key aspects of the spiritual world if I had not experienced certain things that indirectly forced me to better explore reality beyond the physical. For instance, these experiences shifted my perception of the material world, and allowed me to unearth deep secrets about the universe formation.

Indeed, the understanding of the process of the universe formation has been preoccupying human beings for as long as they have existed on Earth. Cosmology is the study of the origin and development of the cosmos, the universe. Toward that end, countless theories have been elaborated and books written to try to explain how the universe was formed. Some of those

CHAPTER 1: INTRODUCTION

theories have been abandoned because they were deemed false after new evidences and theories "contradicted" them or were thought to be "better". Some of the most influential cosmological books ever published were done by Isaac Newton around the 18th century and by Albert Einstein in the 20th century.

When I was writing some of the first chapters of my books on the origin of the universe, of life, and of chemicals in 2017, I understood that most of the contemporary theories in cosmology were based on the relativity work of Albert Einstein. Because I was dissatisfied with the scientific books written on the origin of life, I spent 12 years (2013-2025) investigating the question and writing books on it. However, during my inquisition, I was shocked to learn that some top secrets about the creation of the universe were revealed to the Jews, not only in the Bible, but also in other Jewish books, but unfortunately, these books were rejected by some leaders, and therefore not included in the Bible, although other books in the Bible refer to them. Some of these lost books are the Books of Enoch.

In my book *"Reconciling Science and Creation Accurately"*, I initially wrote about the Books on Enoch, but as the details grew, the information became too much to be put in that book. Moreover, I realized that most believers in the God of Israel still deny the authenticity of the Books of Enoch. I also discovered that, while many people want to know deep things about creation, even in the so-called rejected and lost scriptures, others perceive these mysteries as heresy because these people were told, maybe by their church elders, that such books are heresy.

Therefore, these people have not ventured into checking, reading, reviewing, and assessing for themselves these rejected books excluded from the Bible—some of which are very authentic, but too supernatural for those who compiled the Bible, and who just discarded them because they could not explain or understand them! Consequently, to avoid diluting the message in *"Reconciling Science and Creation Accurately"* and to avoid confusing my readers, I refrained from talking much about them in that book I wrote for the Christians and anyone else interested in understanding Biblical creation.

However, due to the massive amount of information I found in the lost books, particularly the Books of Enoch, and how they influenced and guided me during my search for the real origin of the universe, I decided to reveal a few things about them, hoping that those who wish could follow up for themselves. Furthermore, without the Books of Enoch, many questions which answers I could not find in the Bible could still be staying with me unanswered up until today. In other words, my understanding of the spiritual world was enlightened by the writing of Enoch.

As I was reading and investigating the Books of Enoch in 2015, I learned about and read many other pseudepigraphic scriptures including the Books of Adam and Eve, the Book of Jasher (cited in 2 Samuel 1:18 and Joshua 10:13),

ORIGIN OF THE SPIRITUAL WORLD

and the Book of Jubilees. I therefore bought the Encyclopedia of the lost and rejected scriptures (Lumpkin, 2010), and, many times, I read all of the rejected books in it.

During the process, I learned that the Books of Adam and Eve were also written by Enoch, reportedly between 200-300 BC. Knowing that Enoch lived thousands of years before the Common Era, I understood that, the reported publication date of the Books of Adam and Eve may be the date that they were transcribed and no longer transmitted only through the oral tradition, but also through writing.

Some of the other lost or hidden books were known by Biblical patriarchs. For instance, the Book of Jubilees revealed that Abraham was aware and familiar with the Book of Enoch (Jubilees 21:5-12). In the Book of Jubilees, Abraham told his children that he learned certain things he taught them from the words of Enoch. The third Book of Enoch also explained how Moses was aware of the writings of Enoch, and how Enoch even taught Moses (3 Enoch 48).

My goal here is not to question the authenticity of those books, but to report some intriguing things or information I found in them. For, they answered many questions I had before and during my writing of books on the origin of the universe, of chemicals, and of life (see www.Israel120.com/books). In this book, I will not repeat the information I handled in my other books, but I will focus on mysteries revealed in the lost and rejected scriptures, mainly the pseudepigrapha, NOT the Apocrypha.

So you clearly know how I got here, I will first explain my initial encounter with the Books of Enoch, without which, I would have probably missed the universe origin. Then, I will describe some key stories they contain about creation and the spiritual world. After that, I will talk about mysteries in the Books of Adam and Eve, and others.

As you read this book, you will get a trove of untold information on the spiritual world. Instead of guessing or using fake or unrealistic stories, I will help you understand the origin and functioning of the spiritual world by properly analyzing and guiding you through what was revealed in the hidden books that the elites did not want the public to know for thousands of years. If you are ready for this adventure, let me first start with my discovery of the Books of Enoch.

1.2. How I first learned about the lost and rejected scriptures that people have hidden for millennia–were these books hidden because they were warring against the Bible?

Religion has played a significant role in human invention and interpretation of cosmology. For example, the Biblical book of Genesis (written by Moses) gave a synopsis of how God created the universe. Some Judaic books that

CHAPTER 1: INTRODUCTION

addressed creation were lost, rejected, and classified as secrets by the patriarchs, but they were later discovered or made known to the public. Some of those books are called pseudepigrapha and were well known to Jews even before the birth of Jesus Christ, whom most of the Jews don't accept as their Messiah; yet Jesus Christ himself claimed to be the Messiah. Some of these pseudepigrapha books are the "Books of Enoch", which, as the name indicates, were written by Enoch.

Also called Enock, Enoch was the great-grandfather of Noah. The Book of Genesis revealed that *"Enoch who lived for 365 years, continually walked with God, then he was not, because God took him"* (Genesis 5:21-24). The book of Enoch was even quoted in the New Testament by Jude, the brother of Jesus Christ. If Jude, the brother of Jesus, was aware of the book and even quoted it, it is certain that Jesus also knew it and may have approved of it. Otherwise, Jesus could have advised his own brother, Jude, who is also one of the 12 disciples, not to read it and furthermore not to quote it. Those who carefully read the Books of Enoch may even think or realize that Jesus Christ knew and was quoting them in his revolutionary preaching. In other words, most of the sermons of Jesus in the New Testament were like quotes from the Books of Enoch.

I first learned about the existence of the Book of Enoch around mid-2015 during a live prophetic conference hosted by a famous American prophetic pastor I followed online around 2011-2017. It was during a speech given by an expert of UFOs who was giving a conference (hosted by the aforementioned pastor) that I first heard about the first Book on Enoch. At that time, I was already working on the origin of the universe, and I had already collected most of the raw data available on celestial bodies. I was excited by what that speaker said about the first book of Enoch, as it seemed to contain materials that may answer some questions I was pondering on.

Soon after the aforementioned-speech on UFOs, I quickly searched for the Book of Enoch online. I found it and I downloaded it the same day. Then, I started reading it right away. Soon, I noticed that there is more than one book of Enoch. I also discovered that there are many other rejected books.

Because I noticed that other scriptures were lost, I went ahead and bought the Encyclopedia of the Lost and Rejected Scriptures, which not only contains the Books of Enoch, but also many other hidden books.

As I started reading it, I found a lot of mind-blowing cosmological data in it. Additionally, it contains a lot of materials that go beyond the understanding of a mere human being. I discovered that there are three books of Enoch:
- "1 Enoch", also called the "Book of Enoch", "The Ethiopic Book of Enoch", "The Lost Book of Enoch", or the "Ethiopic Enoch";
- "2 Enoch", also called "The Second Book of Enoch", "Slavonic

ORIGIN OF THE SPIRITUAL WORLD

Enoch", "The Secrets of Enoch", "The Book of the Secrets of Enoch", or "The Slavonic Secrets of Enoch"; and
- "3 Enoch", also called "The Third Book of Enoch", "The Book of the Palaces", "The Book of Rabbi Ishmael the High Priest", "The Revelation of Metatron", or "The Hebrew Book of Enoch".

I read all three books of Enoch many times. Although I did not comprehend all of their content, I did not say anything negative about them. I then began seeking ways to authenticate them and ensure that their content is true. Around the time I started reading the book of Enoch in 2015, I discovered a well-known African prophet.

Prior to discovering that prophet, I was working on Noah's flood and the separation of the continents and found through a mathematic demonstration that Heaven, where is the throne of God sits, is above the North Pole. During one of his live services in Africa in 2015, the aforementioned prophet said that the Book of Enoch is authentic and that Heaven is located above the North. Although this statement of the prophet may sound weird to some people, it meant a lot for me as it was like a confirmation of certain things I was working one.

Two and half years after I wrote the first draft of this book you are reading now, on October 1st, 2020, I was browsing through the YouTube Channel of another renowned African prophet, I came across a teaching he did more than 4 years earlier about the revelation of Enoch. That prophet also confirmed that the Books of Enoch are authentic, but were rejected because they are too accurate and contain information that some people wanted to hide. By that time, I had already read the Book of Enoch more than 7 times and had also already determined in my mind its accuracy.

Then, on Tuesday October 20th, 2020, while another famous African prophet was talking to me over the phone one on one, he mentioned the name of 3 angels, 2 of which I had read about only in the Books of Enoch, therefore indirectly confirming to me the authenticity of these books without me even bringing them up.

As time passed by, although I had heard other preachers (including renowned prophets) talk about the Books of Enoch, I felt like most of them did not read the 3 versions of this book, nor did they understand the scientific implication of these books. I also realized that these books also back up many scientific data that most scientists were unable to explain because these scientists laid wrong hypotheses on the formation of the universe and they did not implicate God, the Creator.

It fascinated me that the book of Genesis written by Moses is an abstract of the detailed cosmology in the Books of Enoch. In fact, according to the Hebrew Book of Enoch, Enoch taught Moses at Mount Sinai where he received the commandments from God. Since the Books of Enoch tremendously agree with the preaching of Jesus Christ, which most Jews

CHAPTER 1: INTRODUCTION

denied, I was not surprised that these books were rejected by Orthodox Jews. That may explain why the Jews did not add them to the Tanakh (Old Testament). Consequently, many of the patriarchs who compiled the Bible, thought that the Books of Enoch were unauthentic and, therefore, they did not add them to the Bible. However, some Bible versions such as the Ethiopian Orthodox Bible contain at least the first Book of Enoch. I was not surprised to discover in 2024 that the Essenes—Jews that were expecting the birth of Jesus just as it happened and who, about 2000 years ago, embraced Him as the Messiah, even before Christianity was born—treasured the Books of Enoch, a fact that can explain why fragments of these books were found among the holy grail of the Dead Sea Scrolls in the 20th century! I will come back to the significance of this discovery in other books. To be informed, sign up for my newsletter at Israel120.com/newsletter.

Many translations exist for the Books of Enoch.
- For 1 Enoch, I used two translations:
  - a) Translation by M. Knibb in the S.O.A.S. Library at the University of London and
  - b) the Translation by Joseph B. Lumpkin.
- For 2 Enoch, I used two translations:
  - Translation by Joseph B. Lumpkin and
  - Translation by W.R. Morfill edited by Henry Frowde.
- For 3 Enoch, I used the translation by Joseph B. Lumpkin.

Unless otherwise specified, throughout this book, the translation I mostly used is that of Joseph B. Lumpkin. I occasionally used the translation by Henry Frowde. In contrast, wherever I quoted the Bible in this book, I used the Tree of Life Version (TLV) and the King James Version (KJV).

After reading the three Books of Enoch, I did not see anything contradicting the Bible. They contain spiritual materials that cannot be comprehended by people who are not prophetic and who cannot see things beyond the physical. These books greatly addressed the spiritual world more than any other book I have ever read.

Here, my goal is to present some of the data I found in them and which I believe are fundamental knowledge that needs to be considered, while trying to scientifically explain the origin of the spiritual world and of the universe from a Judeo-Christian perspective that considers God as the Creator. However, here, I will not give a full account of the cosmological or astronomical stories in the Books of Enoch, but I will focus on key facts related to the formation of the universe, the movement of celestial bodies on the one hand, and on the other hand, I will use these books to explain the origin, formation, role, and organization of angels, etc. This book will help you to see how the formation of the universe was known by Jewish patriarchs long before the foundation of modern science. By the way, throughout my writing, wherever you see "universe-origin", please know that I meant "origin of the universe" or "the origin of the universe". Likewise, wherever you see "life-origin", please understand that I meant "origin of life" or "the origin of life". In the same manner, wherever I mentioned "chemicals-origin", please know that I am referring to "origin of chemicals" or "the origin of chemicals".

Countless books talk about the origin of the spiritual world, of the universe and of life, but this amazing book is the first and the only one that has undeniably explained how the formation of the universe and everything in it (including the spiritual and the spiritual things) was truly revealed in the rejected and hidden scriptures such as the Books of Enoch and others. In *"Origin of the Spiritual World"*, you will:

- Discover deep rejected secrets that have prevented humankind from unearthing the beginning of the spiritual world and of the universe
- Plainly see the scientific proof (hidden in scriptures) of the formation of the Earth, the Moon, and the Sun in a matter of days, a historic revelation that bizarrely and shockingly matches the scientific data as scientifically proved in *"From Science to Bible's Conclusions"*, a popular book written by Dr. Nathanael-Israel Israel
- Properly use the lost and rejected scriptures to articulate the process by which the universe and its spiritual components were formed, and use that insight to improve your understanding of the Bible, innovate in your domain of interest, and improve your life perpetually
- Empower and align yourself with the historic breakthrough that has done what no other discovery has ever done: accurately unlock and decode mysteries concerning the origin of the cosmos and its content using scientific keys revealed in ancient scriptures that some elites have concealed (*Science180.com*/pseudepigraphic)
- Discover and apprehend the complex formation of the spiritual world, of the universe, and of life without leaving out the challenging questions that people of all ages have been struggling to answer for thousands of years, while the answers were hidden
- Find more joy in life through a clear interpretation of old and fresh revelations about the creation of the universe astonishingly backed by modern science, which some people wrongly think opposes the Bible
- Make a difference and blaze new trails for those who depend on your leadership

If you believe in God, have some origin-related questions which answers you cannot find anywhere, not even in the Bible, and if you want to tap into historically neglected revelations to answer fundamental universe and life questions, then you have the right book in front of you.

CHAPTER 1: INTRODUCTION

By the way, for those who don't know me yet, I would like to inform you that I, Nathanael-Israel Israel, happen to be the discoverer of the historic mathematical equations that scientifically demonstrated that the Earth was formed 2.82 days, the Moon 3.32 days, and the Sun 3.69 days after the beginning of the universe, therefore confirming the Biblical account of creation that revealed about 3500 years ago that the formation of the Earth was completed on the 3rd day, while that of the Moon and the Sun was completed on the 4th day of creation. I am fortunate to be referred to as the "Undisputable Specialist of all Questions at the Intersection of Science and Biblical Creation". You can learn more about me at Israel120.com.

As you read this book, your mind will open up to a new perspective that will transform your life.

'Science180 Academy' Success Strategy:
SCIENCE180 BOOKS THAT WILL HELP YOU!

I, Nathanael-Israel Israel, broke down my discovery about the formation of the universe into many books so that you, the readers, can pick the ones that correspond to your needs and interests without disappointing you or wasting your precious time. These books come in many versions (e.g. scientific version, public version, chemical version, biological version, biblical or prophetic version, pseudepigraphic version, and a children's version) targeting people according to their expertise, educational background, and interests as briefed below:

1. "TURBULENT ORIGIN OF THE UNIVERSE"
Learn more at Science180.com/scientific

2. "RECONCILING SCIENCE AND CREATION ACCURATELY"
Learn more at Science180.com/biblical

3. "TURBULENT ORIGIN OF CHEMICAL PARTICLES"
Learn more at Science180.com/chemical

4. "ORIGIN OF THE SPIRITUAL WORLD"
Learn more at Science180.com/pseudepigrapha

5. "FROM SCIENCE TO BIBLE'S CONCLUSIONS"
Learn more at Science180.com/public

6. "TURBULENT ORIGIN OF LIFE"
Learn more at Science180.com/life

7. "HOW BABY UNIVERSE WAS BORN"
Learn more at Science180.com/childrensecular

8. "HOW GOD CREATED BABY UNIVERSE"
Learn more at Science180.com/children

9. "SCIENCE180 ACCURATE SCIENTIFIC PROOF OF GOD"
Learn more at Science180.com/godproof

If you want to have the entire big picture of my discovery of the origin of the universe, life, and chemicals, and to enlighten your life and career, then get all or some of these books at Science180.com/books

CHAPTER 2: ENOCH'S JOURNEY TO THE 10TH HEAVEN AND THINGS HE OBSERVED BEFORE ARRIVING THERE

CHAPTER 2

SHOCKING SECRETS THAT ENOCH, THE MAN WHO WALKED WITH GOD, SAW ON HIS JOURNEY FROM THE EARTH TO THE EXTREMITIES OF THE WHOLE UNIVERSE ... (AND HOW THEY CAN BENEFIT YOU)

2.1. How God sent angels to take Enoch to heaven and show him visions of the creation of the universe

The Books of Enoch detailed the life of Enoch and how God revealed things to him. The books recount that, one day, as Enoch was sleeping on his bed, angels appeared to him and commissioned him to prepare for a trip to heaven. This was the beginning of the journey that led him to see heavens after going through some transformations that allowed him to survive the conditions of the environment he visited. The visit happened when Enoch was about 365 years old, which was shortly before God removed him from the dwellings of men and took him to heaven. It is important to notice that Enoch lived before the Great Flood. In those days, people were living hundreds of years. For instance, Adam lived 930 years, while Methuselah (the son of Enoch born about 200 years before Enoch was taken to heaven) lived 970 years. It was after the Great Flood that God limited the human life span to 120 years of age. Yet, there are some few records of people living past 120 years of age. In 1 Enoch and 3 Enoch, a clear account was not given to how God sent angels to take Enoch and show him secrets. However, in 2 Enoch, the story explained how Enoch's vision started:

2 Enoch 1:1 There was a wise man and a great craftsman, and the Lord formed a love for him and received him, so that he should see the highest dwellings and be an eye-witness of the wise and great and inconceivable and unchanging realm of God Almighty, and of the

ORIGIN OF THE SPIRITUAL WORLD

very wonderful and glorious and bright and manifold vision of the position of the Lord's servants, and of the inaccessible throne of the Lord, and of the degrees and manifestations of the spiritual (nonphysical) hosts, and of the unspeakable ministration of the multitude of the elements, and of the various apparition and singing of the host of Cherubim which is beyond description, and of the limitless light. 2 At that time, he said, when my one hundred and sixty-fifth year was completed, I [Enoch] begat my son Methuselah. 3 After this I lived two hundred years and finished of all the years of my life three hundred and sixty-five years. 4 On the first day of the month, **I was in my house alone and was resting on my bed and slept. 5 And when I was asleep, great distress came up into my heart, and I was weeping with my eyes in sleep, and I could not understand what this distress was, or what was happening to me. 6 And there appeared to me two very large men, so big that I never saw such on earth.** *Their faces were shining like the sun, their eyes were like a burning light, and from their lips fire was coming out. They were singing. Their clothing was of various kinds in appearance and was purple. Their wings were brighter than gold, and their hands whiter than snow. 7 They were standing at the head of my bed and began to call me by my name.* **8 And I arose from my sleep and clearly saw the two men standing in front of me. 9 And I greeted them and was seized with fear and the appearance of my face was changed to terror, and those men said to me: 10 Enoch, have courage and do not fear. The eternal God sent us to you, and you shall ascend today with us into heaven, and you shall tell your sons and all your household all that they shall do without you on earth in your house and let no one seek you until the Lord returns you to them.** *11 And I hurried to obey them and went out of my house, and went to the doors, as I was ordered, and I summoned my sons Methuselah and Regim and Gaidad and explained to them all the marvels the men had told me.*
2 Enoch 2:1 Listen to me, my children, I do not know where I will go, or what will befall me. So now, my children, I tell you, do not turn from God in the face of that which is empty or prideful, which did not make heaven and earth, for these shall perish along with those who worship them, and may the Lord make your hearts confident in the fear (respect) of him. **And now, my children, let no one consider seeking me, until the Lord returns me to you.**

That was the message Enoch relayed to his children before the holy angels took him for the journey to the dwelling of God, passing many heavens. After leaving the Earth, Enoch observed many things before reaching the presence of God. One of the first things Enoch saw was an "ether" in space. He also observed how angels rule the stars in the universe, how the movement of the Sun is associated with the blowing of winds and the effect of four stars. He observed that the light of the Sun is kindled by angels, and the circuit and great circle of the Sun. He remarked that stars and celestial bodies were formed from a fire. He noticed that winds are the pillar of the universe and they move stars and the moon. He detailed the winds of earth and what comes out of them. He observed that winds blow under the wings of angels and that the Sun and the Moon are bound together by an

CHAPTER 2: ENOCH'S JOURNEY TO THE 10TH HEAVEN AND THINGS HE OBSERVED BEFORE ARRIVING THERE

oath. He remarked that one star in the universe is bigger than the others. He also revealed that the orbital parameters of the Moon and the Earth will change while the Sun will become brighter in the last days. He noticed that celestial bodies move in circular chariot. He also observed how celestial bodies move according to their leaders. Finally, he also talked about how God stretched the heavens. After I detail each of these things Enoch observed during his journey to the presence of God, I will reveal what he was told about the creation of the universe once he met God, after visiting or passing through 9 heavens beforehand.

'Science180 Academy' Success Strategy
SCIENCE180 CONSULTING

Because Science180's trainings, seminars, or strategic work sessions (through which it transfers skills and training solutions) are great, some customers want to go even deeper on a long-term, sustainable basis. That is where Science180 Consulting, one-on-one consulting, and mentoring (that some people may prefer calling coaching programs) comes in. That is where Science180 can truly change people's behavior on a long-term basis according to their specific needs. With Science180 Consulting, you will discover and understand the deep secrets of the formation of the universe, life, and chemicals around you. Hear Dr. Nathanael-Israel Israel's personal selection and teaching on key topics that will help you break the code of the universe formation and functioning. All strategically designed to enlighten you, guide you to navigate and filter the massive data collected on the universe and its content so you know how to answer the world's most challenging origin questions, remove any scientific and philosophical cataracts that may be blocking you, and help bring you many steps closer to your best life today and forever. Science180 Consulting will train you, transfer unconventional skills to you and change your behavior so you go deeper. To get started today or to learn more, go to Science180Consulting.com.

2.2. Ether in space

One of the first things Enoch saw was the ether in space. Indeed, after appearing to Enoch, the holy angels took him on their wings and lifted him up to the first heaven. Not long after Enoch left the Earth, he said he saw something described as an ether:

*2 Enoch 3:1 It came to pass, when Enoch had finished speaking to his sons, that the angels took him on to their wings and lifted him up on to the first heaven and placed him on the clouds. And there I (Enoch) looked, and again **I looked higher, and saw the*** *ether, and they placed me on the first heaven and showed me a very large sea, bigger than the earthly sea.*

This story may be where some scientists got their inspiration about ether in space. The existence of ether in space was debated for centuries until the time of Albert Einstein when his theory of relativity seemed to slow down the enthusiasm scientists had in using it in their cosmological theories. Therefore, since the time of Albert Einstein, few theories have focused on the presence of ether in space. However, Enoch did not describe what the ether he saw looked like or what it is made of.

The sea that Enoch saw here should not be confused with the water in the oceans of earth. However, it can be the sea of water that God stored in space after creation and which He poured onto the earth during the time of Noah to flood and kill the civilization of Cain. As of today, scientists cannot see that sea anymore because its water could have already been poured onto the earth like rain. The very large sea that Enoch saw could also be a sea of water present somewhere beyond the Solar System.

2.3. Angels rule the stars in the universe

Before Enoch reached the throne of God, he saw a lot of things in space, some of which are the movements of stars. He found that the movement and services of stars are controlled by angels, meaning that spiritual forces are behind their movement and characteristics. According to Enoch, 200 angels ruled these stars. This account may not apply to all of the stars in the universe, as until this point of the story, Enoch was only referring to the first heaven:

2 Enoch 4:1 They brought the elders and rulers of the stellar orders in front of me, and showed me **two hundred angels, who rule the stars** *and services of the stars to the heavens and fly with their wings and come round all those who sail.*

The fact that stars are ruled by angels is a proof that their dynamics and cinematic cannot be explained by mere physics. For certain things are so tiny that they can never be apprehended using physical means. That is one of the reasons scientists who do not believe in God cannot explain the origin of the universe.

2.4. Movement of the Sun is associated with the blowing of winds and accompanied by four stars

According to Enoch, winds are the engine that is moving the Sun:

2 Enoch 11:1 Those men took me, and led me up on to the fourth heaven, and showed me the entire succession of activities, and all the rays of the light of sun and moon. 2 And I measured their progression, and compared their light, and saw that the sun's light is greater than the moon's. 3 **Its circle and the wheels on which it goes always is like the wind passing with very amazing speed with no** *rest day or night. 4 Its egress* [the action of going out of or leaving a place] *and ingress* [the action or fact of

CHAPTER 2: ENOCH'S JOURNEY TO THE 10TH HEAVEN AND THINGS HE OBSERVED BEFORE ARRIVING THERE

going in or entering] *are **accompanied by four huge stars, and each star has a thousand stars under it,** to the right of the sun's wheel there are four thousand stars and to the left are four thousand, altogether eight thousand, going out with the sun continually. 5 And by day fifteen groups of ten thousand angels attend it, and by night there were a thousand.*

Four huge stars go with the Sun and each of them affects the movement of a thousand stars. This suggests that a family of 4 stars is affecting the movement of the Sun and each of them controlled other stars. Some of these 4 stars can be in the Milky Way Galaxy. The eight thousand stars that are mentioned to go out with the Sun all the times may be referring to real stars, some celestial bodies in the Solar System or beyond. For in most ancient writings, anything that shines in the sky was called a star. These statements suggest that the movement of the Sun is affected by other stars, which, at their turn, are affected by other stars. In other words, the movements of stars in the universe are connected according to their system. Just as the Sun affects the movement of celestial bodies in the Solar System, the movements of other stars are probably affected by stars bigger than them, and so on and so forth. This description may allude to how celestial bodies are connected by systems that depend on one another. The movement of the Sun in the sky is explained as follows:

2 Enoch 48:1 That the sun goes along the seven heavenly circles, which are the appointment of one hundred and eighty-two thrones, that it goes down on a short day, and again one hundred and eighty-two, that it goes down on a big day, and he has two thrones on which he rests, revolving hither and thither above the thrones of the months, from the seventeenth day of the month Tsivan it goes down to the month Thevan, from the seventeenth of Thevan it goes up. 2 And thus it goes close to the earth, then the earth is glad and makes grow its fruits, and when it goes away, then the earth is sad, and trees and all fruits have no florescence. 3 All this he measured, with good measurement of hours, and fixed a measure by his wisdom, of the visible (physical) and the invisible (spiritual).

The seven circles on which the Sun goes may be referring to some details about its orbit or movement in space. Science may have not identified these heavenly circles and what they mean.

2.5. Winds are the pillars of the universe and they move stars, the earth, and the moon

As I kept investigating the origin of the universe, I realized that, to fully explain the formation of the Solar System and the universe, a deep explanation must be given to the origin and role of winds. The Books of Enoch also deeply explained the winds in the universe and how the Sun affects the movements of some celestial bodies. Indeed, Enoch explained how winds played a crucial role during the formation of the universe and the maintenance of the movement of celestial bodies. As an example, the cosmological story in the Ethiopic Book of Enoch begins with winds and their crucial role during the creation of the universe (1 Enoch 18:1-5).

1 Enoch *18:1 And I* [Enoch] *saw the storehouses of all the winds, and I saw how with them He* [GOD] *has adorned all creation, and I saw the foundations of the Earth. 18.2 And I saw the cornerstone of the Earth. And I saw the four winds which support the Earth and the sky. 18.3 And I saw how the winds stretch out the height of Heaven, and how they position themselves between Heaven and Earth; they are the Pillars of Heaven. 18.4 And I saw the winds which turn the sky and cause the disc of the Sun and all the stars to set. 18.5 And I saw the winds on the Earth which support the clouds and I saw the paths of the Angels. I saw at the end of the Earth; the firmament of Heaven above.*

These verses suggest that certain types of winds played a crucial role in the formation and/or maintenance of the Earth, and other celestial bodies in the universe. According to the story, four winds support the Earth and the sky. Winds stretched out the height of Heaven. They are positioned in the universe in a specific way. Some winds on the Earth support the clouds. As the pillars of Heaven, they affect the makeup of the universe. Some winds account for the movement of the Sun and other stars. Therefore, the dynamics of winds must play a crucial role in cosmology.

More details about the movement of the Sun are given in 1 Enoch 72. For instance, the movement of the Sun is highly connected to the blowing of winds: *"The wind blows the chariots on which the Sun ascends, and the Sun goes down in the sky and returns through the north in order to reach the east"* (1 Enoch 72:5). Can this statement be alluding to the wobbling of the Sun?

Enoch also described how the Moon is moved by winds (1 Enoch 73:1-3):

"1 Enoch *73:1 And after this law, I saw another law, for the lesser light, named the moon. 73.2 And its disc is like the disc of the Sun, and the wind blows its chariot on which it rides, and in fixed measure light is given to it"*.

According to this statement, Enoch already said that light is not transmitted continually, but by measure.

CHAPTER 2: ENOCH'S JOURNEY TO THE 10TH HEAVEN AND THINGS HE OBSERVED BEFORE ARRIVING THERE

> **'Science180 Academy' Success Strategy**
> **SCIENCE180 SEMINARS**
>
> People whose awareness is raised by Science180 usually ask to go deeper or wonder "what's else?". That is one of the reasons Science180 trains them through strategic work sessions (during seminars or training sessions) that transfer customizable skills and solutions to them. Science180 Seminars are client-centered and tailored to strongly engage the clients so they maximize the discovery of and the tapping into new opportunities, and exponentially outperform their expectations. Science180 offers customizable seminars that can be labeled as a colloquy, conference, consultation, discussion, forum, keynote speech, lecture, lesson, meeting, symposium, summit, study group, tutorial, workshop or working section accordingly on any topic related to:
> - Universe-origin for scientists and mathematicians, philosophers, laypeople, and the general public
> - Universe-origin or universe creation for believers
> - Life-origin for life scientists, for all other scientists, and for believers
> - Chemical-origin for scientists
> - Universe-origin seminars for children
> - Universe and life-origin for pseudepigraphic believers
>
> As you contact us with your needs, we can customize your program accordingly. Learn more at Science180Seminars.com.

2.6. Characteristics of the winds of earth

Enoch saw 12 gates from which proceed winds toward the Earth (1 Enoch 76:1): "*At the ends of the earth I saw* **twelve doors open to all quarters of heaven, from which the winds** *go out and blow over the earth*". At the North of the Earth, he saw three gates from which blow winds causing: cold, hail, frost, snow, dew, and rain. At the West of the Earth, he saw three gates and at the East, he also saw three gates. At the South, he saw three gates out of which proceed dew, rain, and winds (1 Enoch 34-36). Through other "*four gates come winds of blessing and peace; whereas from others, come winds of punishment*" (1 Enoch 76:4). These winds were divided to blow over the earth and Enoch even saw the "*closed storehouses from which the winds are distributed*" (1 Enoch 41:3-5).

The "*doors of the winds are calculated for each according to the power of the wind*" (1 Enoch 60:12), meaning that the size of the gates of these winds vary and depend on the strength of these winds. The existence of those doors suggests that the winds are not blowing anyhow, but very orderly.

Sketch of the winds around the Earth according to the Book of Enoch (1 Enoch 76)

Credit: Dr. Nathanael-Israel Israel / www.Science180.com

Type of winds	Type / Inclination of winds	Characteristics of these winds (what come out of them)
East winds	East - South	desolation, drought, heat, and destruction (1 Enoch 76: 5)
	East - Toward the middle or center	rain, fruitfulness, prosperity and dew (1 Enoch 76: 6)
	East - North	cold and drought (1 Enoch 76: 6)
South winds	South - East	hot wind (1 Enoch 76: 7)
	South - Toward the middle or center	pleasant fragrances, dew, rain, prosperity, and life/health (1 Enoch 76: 8)
	South - West	dew, rain, locusts, and devastation (1 Enoch 76: 9)
North winds	North - East	dew, rain, locusts, and devastation (1 Enoch 76: 10)
	North - Toward the middle or center	rain, dew, life, and prosperity (1 Enoch 76: 11)
	North - West	mist, hoarfrost, snow, rain, dew, and locusts (1 Enoch 76: 11)
West winds	West - North	dew, rain, hoarfrost, cold, snow, and frost (1 Enoch 76: 12)
	West - Toward the middle or center	dew, rain, prosperity and blessing (1 Enoch 76: 13)
	West - South	drought, devastation, burning and destruction (1 Enoch 76: 13-14)

Enoch also told his children that the winds on earth are regulated in a way that prevents them from hurting the earth.

2 Enoch 40:8 And I wrote the resting-places of the winds and observed and saw how their key holders bear weighing-scales and measures; first, they put them in (one) weighing-scale, then in the other the weights and let them out according to measure cunningly over the whole earth, lest by heavy breathing they make the earth to rock.

2.7. Winds blow under the wings of angels

Though the winds in the universe may be guided by several spiritual agents, 3 Enoch 23 explained that some winds blow under the wings of Cherubim. Cherubim are groups of angels who directly attend to God. God has used them to guard the Garden of Eden after the fall of Adam and Eve (Genesis 3:24). They are also described as the bearer of the Throne of God (Psalms

CHAPTER 2: ENOCH'S JOURNEY TO THE 10TH HEAVEN AND THINGS HE OBSERVED BEFORE ARRIVING THERE

18:9-10, Psalms 80:1, Psalms 99:1). The Books of Enoch revealed that the winds of the Cherubim go out from under their wings and descend on the globe of the sun. The wind goes toward the south and turns around to the north; it turns around over and over in its course and returns again to its route. And from the orb of the sun the winds return and go down on to the rivers and the seas, then up on the mountains and up on the hills. And from the mountains and hills they return and go down again to the seas and the rivers; and from the seas and rivers, they return and go up to the cities and provinces, ...:

*3 Enoch 23: 1 There are numerous winds blowing under the wings of the Cherubim. There blows "the Brooding Wind", for it is written (Gen. 1:2): "and the wind of God was brooding upon the face of the waters." (2) There blows "the Strong Wind", as it is said (Ex. 14:21): "and the Lord caused the sea to go back by a strong east wind all that night." (3) There blows "the East Wind" for it is written (Ex. 10: 13): "the east wind brought the locusts." (4) There blows "the Wind of Quails for it is written (Num. 9:31): "And there went forth a wind from the Lord and brought quails." (5) There blows "the Wind of Jealousy" for it is written (Num. 5:14): "And the wind of jealousy came upon him." (6) There blows the "Wind of Earthquake" and it is written (I Kings 19:11): "and after that the wind of the earthquake; but the Lord was not in the earthquake." (7) There blows the "Wind of YHWH" [YAHWEH] for it is written (Ex. 37:1): "and he carried me out by the wind of YHWH and set me down." (8) There blows the "Evil Wind" for it is written (I Sam. 14:23): "and the evil wind departed from him." (9) There blows the "Wind of Wisdom" and the "Wind of Understanding" and the "Wind of Knowledge" and the "Wind of the Fear of YHWH" for it is written (Is. 11:2): "And the wind of YHWH shall rest upon him; the wind of wisdom and understanding, the wind of counsel and might, the wind of knowledge and the fear of YHWH." (10) There blows the "Wind of Rain", for it is written (Prov. 25:23) "the north wind brings forth rain." (11) There blows the "Wind of Lightning", for it is written (Jer. 10:13): "he makes lightning for the rain and brings forth the wind out of his storehouses." (12) There blows the "Wind, Which Breaks the Rocks", for it is written (1 Kings 19:11): "the Lord passed by and a great and strong wind (rent the mountains and break in pieces the rocks before the Lord.) (13) There blows the Wind of Assuagement of the Sea", for it is written (Gen. 7:1): "and God made a wind to pass over the earth, and the waters assuaged." (14) There blows the "Wind of Wrath", for it is written (Job 1:19): 'and behold there came a great wind from the wilderness and smote the four corners of the house and it fell." (15) There blows the "Wind of Storms", for it is written (Ps. 148:8): "Winds of the storm, fulfilling his word." (16) And Satan is standing among these winds, for "the winds of the storm" is nothing else but "Satan" and **all these winds do not blow but under the wings of Cherubim, for it is written (Ps. 18.11): "and he rode upon a cherub and flew, yes, and he flew with speed upon wings of the wind." (17) And where do all these winds go? The Scripture teaches us, that they go out from under the wings of the Cherubim and descend on the globe of the sun**, for it is written (Eccl. 1:6): "The wind goes toward the south and turns around to the north; it turns around over and

ORIGIN OF THE SPIRITUAL WORLD

over in its course and the wind returns again to its route." And from the orb of the sun they return and go down on to the rivers and the seas, then up on the mountains and up on the hills, for it is written (Am. 55:13): "For lo, he that forms the mountains and creates the wind." (18) And from the mountains and the hills they return and go down again to the seas and the rivers; and from the seas and the rivers they return and go up to the cities and provinces: and from the cities and provinces they return and go down into the Garden, and from the Garden they return and descend to Eden, for it is written (Gen. 3: 8) "walking in the Garden in the wind (cool) of day." In the middle of the Garden they come together and blow from one side to the other. In the Garden they are perfumed with spices from the Garden in its most remote parts, until the winds again separate from each other. Filled with the odor of the pure spices, the winds bring the aroma from the most remote parts of Eden. They carry the spices of the Garden to the righteous and godly who in time to come will inherit the Garden of Eden and the Tree of life, for it is written (Cant 45:16): "Awake, 0 north wind; and come you south; blow upon my garden and eat his precious fruits."

Because other types of angels also have wings, it is likely that winds blow below their wings too. For instance, in 3 Enoch 24, other types of chariots of God are revealed just like the chariot of Cherubim. In other words, God moves on many angels including Cherubim:

3 Enoch 24: The different chariots of the Holy One, blessed be He. *1 The Holy One blessed be He, has innumerable chariots. He has the "Chariots of the Cherubim", for it is written (Ps. 18:11, 2 Sam 22:11):"And he rode upon a cherub and did fly." (2) He has the "Chariots of Wind", for it is written: "and he flew swiftly upon the wings of the wind." (3) He has the "Chariots of the Swift Cloud", for it is written (Is. 19:1): "Behold, the Lord rides upon a swift cloud: (4) He has "Chariots of Clouds", for it is written (Ex. 19:9): "Lo, I come unto you in a cloud." (5) He has the "Chariots of the Altar", for it is written, "I saw the Lord standing upon the Altar." (6) He has the "Chariots of Ribbotaim", for it is written (Ps. 68:18): "The chariots of God are Ribbotaim; thousands of angels."(7) He has the "Chariots of the Tent", for it is written (Deut. 31:15): "And the Lord appeared in the Tent in a pillar of cloud." (8) He has the "Chariots of the Tabernacle", for it is written (Lev. 1:1): "And the Lord spoke unto him out of the tabernacle." (9) He has the "Chariots of the Mercy-Seat", for it is written (Num. 7:89): "then he heard the Voice speaking unto him from upon the mercy-seat." (10) He has the "Chariots of Sapphire", for it is written (Ex. 24:10): "and there was under his feet a paved street of sapphires." (11) He has the "Chariots of Eagles", for it is written (Ex. 19:4): "I bare you on eagles' wings." It is not Eagles that are not meant here but "they that fly as swiftly as the eagles." (12) He has the "Chariots of a Shout", for it is written: "God is gone up with a shout." (13) He has the "Chariots of Araboth (highest heaven)," for it is written (Ps 68:5): "Praise Him that rides upon the Araboth (highest heaven)." (14) He has the "Chariots of Thick Clouds", for it is written (Ps. 106:3): "who makes the thick clouds His chariot." (15) He has the "Chariots of the Chayoth," for it is written (Ezek. 1:14): "and the Chayoth ran and returned." They run by permission and return by permission, for Shekina is above their heads. (16) He has the "Chariots of*

CHAPTER 2: ENOCH'S JOURNEY TO THE 10TH HEAVEN AND THINGS HE OBSERVED BEFORE ARRIVING THERE

Wheels (Galgallim)", for it is written (Ezek. 10:2): "And he said: Go in between the whirling wheels." (17) He has the "Chariots of a Swift Cherub," for it is written, "riding on a swift cherub." And at the time when He rides on a swift cherub, as he sets one of His feet upon his back, and before he sets the other foot upon his back, he looks through eighteen thousand worlds at one glance. And he perceives and understands and sees into them all and knows what is in all of them, and then he sets down the other foot upon the cherub, for it is written (Ezek. 48:35): "Round about eighteen thousand." How do we know that He looks through every one of them every day? It is written (Ps. 14:2): "He looked down from heaven upon the children of men to see if there were any that understand, that seek after God." (18) He has the "Chariots of the Ophannim", for it is written (Ezek. 10:12): "and the Ophannim were full of eyes round about." (19) He has the "Chariots of His Holy Throne", for it is written (Ps. 67:8): "God sits upon his holy throne" (20) He has the "Chariots of the Throne of Yah (Jah)", for it is written (Ex. 17:16): "Because a hand is lifted up upon the Throne of Jah (Yah)." (21) He has the "Chariots of the Throne of Judgment," for it is written (Is. 5:16): "but the Lord of hosts shall be exalted in judgment." (22) He has the "Chariots of the Throne of Glory", for it is written (Jer. 17:12): "The Throne of Glory, set on high from the beginning, is the place of our sanctuary." (23) He has the "Chariots of the High and exalted Throne", for it is written (Is. 6:1): "I saw the Lord sitting upon the high and exalted throne."

Because they control planets and stars, the movement of angels is likely the source of the force that moves these celestial bodies. Consequently, it would be impossible for a mere scientist who rejects the power of angels to fully understand the magnitude and dynamics of winds, angels, and motions of celestial bodies in the universe.

2.8. Angels kindle the light of the Sun

The thousands of angels that accompanied the Sun were split into groups. Some attend the Sun and others kindle it and set it alight:

2 Enoch 11:6 And six-winged ones go forth with the angels before the sun's wheel into the fiery flames, and a **hundred angels kindle the sun and set it alight**.

This statement implies that the light of the Sun is produced by an angelic kindling, meaning that the production of light by the Sun is not a simple chemical reaction, but a supernatural reaction physically manifested as light. Yet most scientists would argue that the light emitted by the Sun is just a chemical reaction between hydrogen atoms to produce helium, etc. The reaction by or between hydrogen to produce Sun light may just be a physical manifestation of a spiritual reaction handled by angels. In addition to the angels who kindle the Sun, many others guard its flame. Enoch stated that the flames of the Sun are guarded by 400 angels and these flames are more than fire:

2 Enoch 14:2 ... for since the crown of its [Sun] shining is in heaven with the Lord, and **guarded by four hundred angels**, *while the sun goes around on wheel under the earth, ..., and the* **sun flames forth more than fire**.

> **'Science180 Academy' Success Strategy**
> **SCIENCE180 MASTER CLASS**
> Hear the greatest scientific and philosophic lessons from top scientists, philosophers, thinkers, and public figures who have realized historic mistakes they made in life (concerning the origin of the universe, life, and chemicals), and that they corrected thanks to the historic discovery of Nathanael-Israel Israel, the world's first 180Scientist who founded Science180 and who is known as the one who truly decrypted the universe-origin for the first time. In their own words, these renowned personalities share with the world key lessons they have learned in life and how people can learn from their experiences to improve lives instead of repeating their mistakes that many people still ignore at their own perils. To learn more, contact us at Science180.com/contact.

2.9. Sun's circuit and great circle

During his journey to the dwelling of God, Enoch observed that every 28 years, the Sun finishes a circuit:

2 Enoch 15:3 For this reason the sun is a great creation, **whose circuit lasts twenty-eight years***, and begins again from the beginning.*

Although no detail is given to the meaning of the spatial events associated with the 28-year circuit, some commentators pointed out that it is a form of perpetual calendar linked to leap year. Indeed, it is said that a 28-year cycle is needed for 29 February (the leap year day) to fall on a particular weekday. Furthermore, without much detail, Enoch talked about a great circuit that contains 532 years: *2 Enoch 16:4 Thus, too, the great circle contains five hundred and thirty-two years"*. To my knowledge, the scientific implication of the 28-year cycle and 532-year circuit may not be known yet, for I did not see any reference to them in the scientific literature. But in 2025, I discovered that the 28-year cycle is highly connected to how the years were supposed to be counted according to a certain calendar I will address in my incoming book on the age of the universe.

2.10. Orbit of celestial bodies and oath binding the Sun and the Moon

During this journey to the 10th heaven, Enoch observed that celestial bodies move in circular chariots, which can be alluding to the orbital motion or revolution of celestial bodies or how celestial bodies are moved by something as if they were carried by a chariot (1 Enoch 82:7-9):

1 Enoch 82:7 And the account of it is accurate and the recorded counting thereof is exact; for the luminaries, and months and festivals, and years and days, has Uriel shown and

CHAPTER 2: ENOCH'S JOURNEY TO THE 10TH HEAVEN AND THINGS HE OBSERVED BEFORE ARRIVING THERE

*revealed to me, to whom the Lord of the whole creation of the world hath subjected the host of heaven. 8 And he has power over night and day in heaven to cause the light to shine on men via the sun, moon, and stars, and all **the powers of the heaven which revolve in their circular chariots**. 9 And these are the orders of the stars, which set in their places, and in their seasons and festivals and months.*

Furthermore, Enoch also mentioned that, the Sun and the Moon are bound together by an oath and he saw their *"stately orbit, how they do not leave their orbit, and they add nothing to their orbit and they take nothing from it, and they keep faith with each other, in accordance with the oath by which they are bound together"* (1 Enoch 41:6). Knowing that few astronomical terms were known at the days when the Books of Enoch were written (before Common Era), it can be difficult to put into contemporary terms what Enoch meant by *"bound together by an oath"*. However, the binding together by an oath may suggests that the Sun and the moon and likely the other bodies in the Solar System are bound together by a law. Because this statement concerning the oath was mentioned in the middle of the relation concerning winds, it is probable that the thing that connects the celestial bodies may be linked to the winds that are blowing around them.

2.11. One star in the universe is bigger than the others

Among the stars in the universe, one is the largest and it makes its course through the entire world (1 Enoch 75:8-9):

"1 Enoch *75:8 And I saw chariots in Heaven, running through the region above those Gates, in which the stars that never set rotate. 75.9 And **one is bigger than all the others. And it goes round through the whole world**".*

This suggests that one major star may be controlling and/or influencing the movements in the entire universe, and the other stars may depend on it to move and/or to maintain their movement. Just as the planets and asteroids in the Solar System orbit the Sun, it is possible that all bodies in the universe are orbiting by the aforementioned biggest star.

2.12. Enoch's arrival at the 10th Heaven, the dwelling place of God and his transfiguration

Now that I have presented what Enoch saw in space before reaching the dwelling of God, I will now describe what he was told once he met God. After a long journey through space, Enoch was led to the presence of God in the 10th Heaven. Because of the brightness of God's face, Enoch had to be transfigured before being able to withstand His presence. After Enoch journeyed through and learned new things about each of the nine heavens, it was in the tenth heaven that God commanded an angel to show Enoch most of the secrets of creation. Because of the significance of the creation story, I would like to first report what happened to Enoch as he approached the

ORIGIN OF THE SPIRITUAL WORLD

tenth heaven:

2 Enoch 20:1 And those two men lifted me up from there [6th heaven] on to the seventh heaven, and I saw there a very great light, and fiery troops of great archangels, incorporeal forces, and dominions, orders and governments, Cherubim and Seraphim, thrones and many-eyed ones, nine regiments, the Ioanit stations of light, and I became afraid, and began to tremble with great terror, and those men took me, and led me after them, and said to me: 2 Have courage, Enoch, do not fear, and showed me the Lord from afar, sitting on His very high throne. For what is there on the tenth heaven, since the Lord dwells there? 3 **On the tenth heaven is God, in the Hebrew tongue he is called Aravat.** *4 And all the heavenly soldiers would come and stand on the ten steps according to their rank, and would bow down to the Lord, and would then return to their places in joy and bliss, singing songs in the unlimited light with soft and gentle voices, gloriously serving Him.*

2 Enoch 21:1 And the Cherubim and Seraphim standing around the throne, and the six-winged and many-eyed ones do not depart, standing before the Lord's face doing His will, and cover His whole throne, singing with gentle voice before the Lord's face: Holy, holy, holy, Lord Ruler of Sabaoth (Host/ army), heavens and earth are full of Your glory. 2 When I saw all these things, the men said to me: Enoch, thus far we were commanded to journey with you, and those men went away from me and after that I did not see them. 3 And I remained alone at the end of the seventh heaven and became afraid and fell on my face and said to myself: Woe is me. What has befallen me? 4 And the Lord sent one of his glorious ones, the archangel Gabriel, and he said to me: "Have courage, Enoch, do not fear, arise before the Lord's face into eternity, arise and come with me." 5 And I answered him, and said within myself: My Lord, my soul has departed from me due to terror and trembling, and I called to the men who led me up to this place. I relied on them, and it is with them that I can go before the Lord's face. 6 And Gabriel lifted me up like a leaf caught up by the wind, and he placed me before the Lord's face. 7 And I saw the eighth heaven, which is called in the Hebrew tongue Muzaloth (Zodiac), the changer of the seasons, of drought, and of wet, and of the twelve constellations of the circle of the firmament, which are above the seventh heaven. 8 And I saw the **ninth heaven, which is called in Hebrew Kuchavim, where are the heavenly homes of the twelve constellations of the circle of the firmament.**

2 Enoch 22:1 On the tenth heaven, which is called Aravoth, I saw the appearance of the Lord's face, like iron made to glow in fire, and it shone forth and casted out, emitting sparks, and it burned. 2 In a moment of eternity, I saw the Lord's face, but the Lord's face is indescribable, marvelous, and very amazing, and very, very terrible. 3 And who am I to tell of the Lord's unspeakable being, and of his very wonderful face? I cannot tell the amount of his instructions, and the variety of voices. The Lord's throne is very great and not made with hands, and I cannot tell the number of those standing around Him. There were troops of Cherubim and Seraphim, and they sang unceasingly. I cannot tell of his unchanging beauty. Who shall tell of the unpronounceable greatness of His glory? 4 And I felt prone and bowed down to the Lord, and the Lord with His lips said to me: 5 Have courage, Enoch, do not fear, arise, and stand before my face into eternity (stand before my face eternally/ stand before my eternal face.) 6 And the archangel Michael lifted me up,

CHAPTER 2: ENOCH'S JOURNEY TO THE 10TH HEAVEN AND THINGS HE OBSERVED BEFORE ARRIVING THERE

and led me to the Lord's face. 7 And the Lord said to his servants, testing them: Let Enoch stand before My face into eternity, and the glorious ones bowed down to the Lord, and said: Let Enoch go according to Your word. 8 **And the Lord said to Michael: Go and take Enoch and remove his earthly garments, and anoint him with my sweet ointment, and put him into the garments of My glory.** *9 And Michael did as the Lord told him. He anointed me, and dressed me, and the appearance of that ointment is more than the great light, and his ointment is like sweet dew, and its smell mild, shining like the sun's ray, and I looked at myself, and I was transformed into one of his glorious ones. 10 And the Lord summoned one of His archangels, whose name is Pravuil, whose knowledge was quicker in wisdom than the other archangels, who wrote all the deeds of the Lord; and* **the Lord said to Pravuil: Bring out the books from my store-houses, and a reed of quick-writing, and give it to Enoch, and deliver to him the best and comforting books out of your hand.**

Before Enoch could stand in the presence of God, he was transformed. His earthly garments, meaning his earthly body, was removed, and replaced by a glorious garment. By anointing Enoch under God's commandment, Michael put on Enoch certain types of matter that are supernatural, suggesting that matters in heaven are certainly different than those on earth. Of course, the environment in heaven is different than that on earth. Consequently, heavenly matter should not be expected to be the same as earthly ones. After Michael anointed Enoch, God commissioned archangel Pravuil to show him [Enoch] the secrets related to creation. For thirty days and thirty nights, Enoch wrote out all things exactly as Pravuil showed him, and he wrote 366 books (2 Enoch 23:3).

Before I close this chapter, I must underline that, thanks to the Books of Enoch, I understood that there are many types of heavens, and the highest of them is where God resides. *3 **Enoch 24:13 revealed** that Araboth, which may be the same thing as Aravoth or* **Aravat** *(2 Enoch 20:) is the highest heaven.* In contrast, the heavens mentioned in the Biblical account of creation of the Book of Genesis is Shamayim. This misunderstanding of this mysterious nuance can cause some people to think that the heaven mentioned in the Biblical account of creation of Genesis 1:1 was about the whole universe. I provided more details on that in my book called *"Reconciling Science and Creation Accurately"*. In the next chapter, I will provide information about what God told Enoch about the formation of the universe.

'Science180 Academy' Success Strategy:
SCIENCE180 ACADEMY OVERVIEW

Science180 Academy is a training, speaking, consulting, and mentoring program designed to groom and empower people of all backgrounds in the truth about the origin of the universe, life, and chemicals. According to their background and interest, trainees are taught different levels of scientific facts to grasp a deeper understanding of the origin of the universe, how to properly think to unearth mysteries hidden in the massive scientific data collected across the globe, but which is unfortunately less analyzed. If you want to be enlightened and equipped so you can cause positive changes in your respective field of expertise, then Science180 Academy program is for you.

Science180 Academy does not confer college credit, grant degrees, or grade its attendants, participants, or students. It is not an accredited university or college, but is the one-stop-destination for universe-origin, life-origin, and chemicals-origin experts. It is where scientists and laypeople get all their origin-related questions properly answered. It is the only place where the accurate interpretation of the universe-origin, life-origin, and chemicals-origin data matters a lot.

Nathanael-Israel's goal is to give you practicable and undeniable proofs of the formation of the universe so you can be fired up to become the best version of you, and to cause positive changes to your initiatives that will profit you today and forever. For Nathanael-Israel, decoding the origin of the universe and everything in it is not a job, but his life mission, and helping others to fully understand that is his mission. Visit Science180Academy.com today to start.

If you are still wondering if Science180 Academy is for you, let me also inform you that some of Science180's clients and prospects have a profound technical knowledge and background in science, while others don't. Some are creationists (e.g. Science180 creationism, Young Earth creationists, Old Earth creationists, Intelligent design proponents), others are anti-creationists. Some are believers, others are freethinkers (including atheists, humanists, rationalists, agnostics, nontheists, nonreligious, skeptics, nonbelievers, religiously unaffiliated, spiritual-not-religious, ex-believers, and doubters). Regardless of their background, belief, or disbelief, Science180 works with each of these people to figure out their needs, priorities, and the products and services that best fit them. Science180 improves their knowledge, experience, performance, and answer their questions (related to the universe-origin, life-origin, and

CHAPTER 2: ENOCH'S JOURNEY TO THE 10TH HEAVEN AND THINGS HE OBSERVED BEFORE ARRIVING THERE

chemicals-origin) by crafting a personalized program that perfectly matches their interests, needs, and things that are dear and meaningful to them whether it is to:

- Protect yourself and loved ones by keeping all of you secured and empowered with the true knowledge of the origin of the universe
- Have a reliable access to the world's authority on origin-related matters and get your origin questions professionally answered with the truth step-by-step
- Connect with practical tips about how to decode the origin of the universe, life, and chemicals and protect yourself from wrong theories in the literature and the media
- Get inside secrets about how to locate flaws in origin-related theories so you can save time, money, and other resources to improve lives
- Bypass technical knowledge that restricts non-experts from accessing the origin-related truth contained in the massive scientific data, and get to the bottom of scientifically-locked origin-related secrets regardless of your background.
- If you are a teacher, discover tools to better engage with students and introduce them to new ideas
- Scientifically test and know whether there is a God that created the universe or not, and which God it is
- Become the leader that captures the heart of your followers, prospects, and customers craving for an unconventional explanation of the origin of the universe, life, and chemicals
- Free yourself from boring explanations of the origin of the universe, life, and chemicals and embrace the proven theory that opens doors to unparallel opportunities
- Satisfy your burning desire for freedom from beliefs and scientific theories about the universe-origin and life-origin that suffocate you and bind your mind, faith, unbelief, heart, and education
- Challenge the cosmological status quo and embrace the real change that will disrupt the cages that were holding you
- Empower yourself to leave unforgettable marks and to stand tall as a symbol of freedom, power, creativity, and originality in your field of expertise

To register or to learn more, visit Science180Academy.com today.

CHAPTER 3

MISS THIS UNCONVENTIONAL STORY ABOUT THE FORMATION OF THE SPIRITUAL AND PHYSICAL WORLD AND YOU WILL NEVER KNOW THE KEY TO OPEN THE SCIENTIFIC AND BIBLICAL GATE THAT CRACKED THE UNIVERSE-ORIGIN

Many books and theories have been written about the formation of the universe, but none have supernaturally delved into the origin mysteries thousands of years ago as you will read in this chapter and other origin-related books I wrote. For instance, the Book of Genesis talked about the origin of the Earth, the Sun, the Moon, and the life on Earth, but it did not detail the story as I presented below. Because the Books of Enoch were written thousands of years ago, some of the terminologies used may be hard to understand using modern vocabulary, but they carry a message that I discovered to resonate very well with the scientific evidences. Instead of being a scientific demonstration of the origin of the universe, this chapter relayed my comments of the universe formation according to the pseudepigrapha, particularly the Books of Enoch. In other books, I scientifically demonstrated the origin and formation of the universe. Without any delay, let's dive into the ancient story of creation.

3.1. God created the physical world from the spiritual world

When Enoch entered into the presence of God, He made him to sit and then, He revealed secrets to him:

2 Enoch 24:1 And the Lord summoned me, and said to me: Enoch, sit down on my left with Gabriel. 2 And I bowed down to the Lord, and **the Lord spoke to me: Enoch,**

CHAPTER 3: FORMATION OF THE UNIVERSE ACCORDING TO THE HIDDEN SCRIPTURES

beloved, all that you see, all things that are standing finished, I tell you even before the very beginning, I created all things from non-being. I created the visible, physical things from the invisible, spiritual (world). 3 Hear, Enoch, and take in my words, for I have not told My angels My secret, and I have not told them their rise (beginnings), nor My endless realm, nor have they understood my creating, which I tell you today. 4 For **before all things were visible (physical), I alone used to go about in the invisible, spiritual things, like the sun from east to west, and from west to east. 5 But even the sun has peace in itself, while I found no peace, because I was creating all things, and I conceived the thought of placing foundations, and of creating the visible, physical creation** (Translation by Joseph B. Lumpkin).

The same story is rendered a little differently by W.R. Morfill's translation: 2 Enoch 24:1 And the Lord called me and said to me" 'Enoch, sit thou on My left hand with Gabriel.' And I made obeisance to the Lord. 2. And the Lord spake to me: 'Enoch, the things which thou seest at rest and in motion were completed by me. I will tell thee now, even from the first, **what things I created from the non-existent, and what visible things from the invisible**. 3. Not even to My angels have I told My secrets, nor have I informed them of their origin, nor have they understood My infinite creation which I tell thee of today. 4. **For before anything which is visible existed, I alone held my course among the invisible things, like the Sun from the east to the west, and from the west to the east.** 5. But even the sun has rest in himself, but I did not find rest, because I was creating everything. And I planned to lay the foundation and to make the visible creation (Translation by W.R. Morfill and edited by Henry Frowde).

During Enoch's visit to the 10th heaven, God told him that spiritual things were the foundation of material things in the universe. Although God did not tell the angels His secrets related to creation, He shared them with Enoch (2 Enoch 24:3). God is very strategic by making angels very powerful but not well informed about some top secrets. In contrast, He made men knowledgeable, but not as strong as angels. Yet, God Himself is Almighty and omniscient, proving that He does not want to be rivaled, but to be praised and worshiped for what He has done and for Who He is. The Bible revealed that before the fall of Adam and Eve, they were very powerful and had a perfect communion and relationship with God. But when they sinned, their power was removed and, in their search for knowledge, they complicated their own life. Anyway, at the very beginning, God was alone and at one point, he decided to lay the foundation of the world He wanted to create. Part of why God created the world is so He would not be alone. The Bible talks about the fact that God created the world for his own pleasure. He made the Earth so it can be inhabited by human beings who will later inherit heaven and eternally fellowship with God and His Son, Jesus Christ.

ORIGIN OF THE SPIRITUAL WORLD

3.2. Adoil (the first physical body that God created) was fragmentated to birth precursors including that of a light God sent above His throne to be the foundation of things of high or heavenly things

God always existed before creation. As He began creating, something very big called "Adoil" came out of the invisible realm. The creation of "Adoil" is the first stage of creation. Adoil was the precursor of the physical world. "Adoil" is translated by others like the "light of creation", suggesting that the precursors of all matter may have been a type of light or something full of energy:

2 Enoch 25:1 I [God] *commanded in the very lowest parts, that the **visible, physical things should come down from the invisible, spiritual (realm), and Adoil came down very great, and I beheld him, and he had a belly of great light. 2 And I said to him: Become undone, Adoil, and let the visible, physical (universe) come out of you. 3 And he came undone, and a great light came out. And I was in the midst of the great light, and as there is born light from light, there came forth a great age (eon/ space of time), and showed all creation, which I had thought to create. 4 And I saw that it was good. 5 And I placed for myself a throne, and took my seat on it, and said to the light: Go up higher from here and station yourself high above the throne and be a foundation to the highest things. 6 And above the light there is nothing else, and then I rose up and looked up from my throne.* (Translation by Joseph B. Lumpkin)

According to the translation by W.R. Morfill edited by Henry Frowde, here is how the story of 2 Enoch 25 was rendered:

*2 Enoch 25:1 **And I commanded in the depths that visible things should come out of invisible. And out came Adoil very great, and I gazed upon him. And lo! His colour was red, of great brightness. 2. And I said unto him: "Burst asunder, Adoil, and let that which comes from thee be visible". 3. And he burst asunder, and there came forth a great light, and I was in the midst of a great light, and as the light came forth from the light, there came forth the great world, revealing all the creation, which I had purposed to make, and I saw that is was good. 4. And I made for Myself a throne, and sat upon it, and I said to the light: "Go forth on high and be established above My throne and be the foundation for things on high". 5. And there was nothing higher than the light, and as I reclined, I saw it from My throne.* (Translation by W.R. Morfill and edited by Henry Frowde).

According to the dictionary, "Burst asunder" means "break or cause to break open or break apart suddenly and noisily, especially from internal pressure; explode, break or divide into pieces, crack or crash open always of

CHAPTER 3: FORMATION OF THE UNIVERSE ACCORDING TO THE HIDDEN SCRIPTURES

making noise". This suggests that the breaking apart or the fragmentation of Adoil was very noisy, powerful, and has divided the original precursor into pieces. Adoil may have not been 100% light, but light was at least in its "belly". Here, belly could mean the interior or the center of Adoil. This points to the fact that the exterior of Adoil may not have been light, but a material which may have been solid or dark. The existence of light in the belly of Adoil corroborates also the fact that most bodies are hotter on the inside than the outside. For instance, the Earth is hard on the outside, but its inside is believed to be filled with lava.

The birth of light from light suggests that the precursors of various types of lights or bodies filled with lights were born out of the fragmentation of Adoil, their original precursor. Light is one of the first things that God created. God forming "Adoil" in the lowest parts means that Adoil was going through some modifications for other things to come out of it, but God stopped that process to birth the primordial physical world. Out of Adoil came light, which God used as the foundation of things on high. At one point, God made for Himself a throne, and after properly positioning above everything He was creating, He took a seat on it. The statement suggested that God created His throne. God's throne and seat were one of the very first things that God formed.

At this point, I will elaborate on the formation and location of the throne of God. Indeed, God is eternal and has always existed. But everything else has a beginning. For instance, while some people may not believe in this, the pseudepigraphic scriptures suggest that God has not always been sitting on His throne. For His throne was formed at one point during the early stage of the creation of the universe. Although the Bible did not reveal how God created His throne, the second Book on Enoch explained how God created His throne and placed it above everything. According to the Books of Enoch, during all of the ages or times that God existed before creating the universe, He was not sitting on a throne, but created it on the first day of creation. While I may not have bothered trying to figure out the position of the throne or dwelling of God that I have never seen face to face, but that I just believe by faith, I did so, because some scriptures gave some clues. Knowing that the Bible described Jesus's coming to Earth and His return to heaven as a descending and ascending movement, I deduct that the throne of God is above us. But in which direction is that throne? If I could point the direction that could lead to the throne of the dwelling of God, I would refer to the North, from which salvation comes! Although the North Pole of the Earth can be aligned with the direction of the throne of God, the omnipresence and infinite nature of God makes it difficult and impossible to locate His position using just conventional cardinals or coordinates. For instance, instead of being like a location above the universe which can be reached using only one direction, the dwelling of God can also surround the whole universe just as a shell surrounds an egg. Moreover, in *"Reconciling Science and Creation Accurately"*, the Biblical version of my books on the origin of the universe, I explained how the motion (generally counterclockwise) of the celestial bodies matched what would have happened if, sitting on His throne located in a direction of the North Pole, God used His right hand to launch the movement of the precursors of the celestial bodies. For the general motion in which the right hand launches things is counter clockwise. In my books on the origin of the universe, I also explained the processes that were involved so that some bodies move clockwise, while others move counterclockwise and some move chaotically.

Interestingly, God summoned the light that came out of Adoil to move and station itself above the throne of God in a way that nothing else is above that light. The Bible declares that God is light and it makes sense that His throne is covered with light. God made the highest things with that light He positioned above His throne. Here, the highest things can be referring to heavenly things, or heavenly bodies, or heavenly matter, which the Bible described as incorruptible and immortal. The quality of heavenly things is higher than that of earthly materials, which are corruptible and mortal. Because of the variety of heavenly things, God could have modeled the light above the throne in different ways to form different heavenly beings and things.

The fact that God was in the midst of the great light of Adoil suggested to me that, by the time God came out, He may have generated some turbulence in Adoil, therefore communicating a movement to it and to its daughter bodies, which were born from its split and gathering. Knowing the power of God, He could have come out of the middle of Adoil quickly, strongly, forcibly, and energetically, therefore shaking the precursors of the things being formed. Knowing that God created everything in 6 days, it is certain that everything was made quickly. Similarly, when God was coming out of the great lighting in the midst of which He was, He moved very fast. That fast movement should have caused or increased the turbulence of the created things which were going thru some changes to acquire their final shape and characteristics. It is possible that the movement of God to leave the center of Adoil and position Himself in His throne above everything may have shaken the precursors of all created things, therefore pushing them into an initial motion. For it is said that when Adoil came into existence, God was in the middle of the great light. We know that God is in heaven today, meaning that during the creation, He moved above.

It is interesting that God did not decide to stay in the midst of the universe just as He was initially in the great light that came out of Adoil. However, since about 2000 years, the Bible declared that God lives inside believers in the form of the Holy Spirit. However, He does not live inside unbelievers or any other things in the universe. This suggests that Adoil must have been a material of high quality. Otherwise, God would not have used it

CHAPTER 3: FORMATION OF THE UNIVERSE ACCORDING TO THE HIDDEN SCRIPTURES

as the foundation of the highest things, nor stay in it for a while. In other words, the precursor of all matter was very pure. It may be the transformation that the original precursor went through to become various physical matters (e.g. earth matters) that limits matter.

Because the story states that Adoil was formed in the lowest part, it is clear that the domain of God and the world He created are not on the same level. Heaven where God dwells is above the created world. How can one know where God resides? That is what I will handle in the next subchapter.

The wrong interpretation of the story in 2 Enoch 25 can be one of the things that strayed Gnostics. Indeed, according to Gnosticism, God did not really want to create the world, but creation just emanated from God just as light come out of a flame. In contrast to this wrong interpretation, the Bible clearly says that God planned the world before creating it, not by chance, but with a clear design.

3.3. Formation of Archas as Adoil was summoned a second time

The first time God summoned Adoil, many light bodies came out (2 Enoch 25). After that stage, God summoned Adoil again to come forth hard, therefore forming "Archas" (also called *Arkhas*) from a transformation of the preexisting materials of "Adoil".

2 Enoch 26:1 And I summoned the very lowest a second time, and said: **Let Archas come forth hard, and he came forth hard from the invisible,** *spiritual. 2 And Archas came forth, hard, heavy, and very red.* **3 And I said: Be opened, Archas, and let there be born from you, and he came apart,** *and an age came forth, very great and very dark,* **bearing the creation of all lower things,** *and I saw that it was good and said to him: 4* **Go down below, and make yourself solid, and be a foundation for the lower things,** *and it happened and he went down and stationed himself, and became the foundation for the lower things, and* **below the darkness there is nothing else.** (Translation by Joseph B. Lumpkin)

The story above is rendered a little differently by the translation of W.R. Morfill edited by Henry Frowde:

2 Enoch 26:1 And I summoned a second time from the depths and said: 'Let the **solid thing which is visible come forth from the invisible'. And Arkhas came forth firm and heavy and very red.** *2. And I said: 'Be thou divided, O Arkhas, and let that be seen which is produced from thee'. And* **when he was divided, the world came forth,** *very dark and great, bringing the creation of all things below. 3. And I saw that it was good. And I said to him: '***Go thou down and be thou established. And be the foundation of things below'***; and it was so. And it came forth and was established and was a foundation of things below. And* **there was nothing else below the darkness.** (Translation by W.R. Morfill and edited by Henry Frowde).

According to this story, the materials in Adoil were not initially hard, but at one-point, God commanded it to harden and it did. Additionally, the notion of weight and color was introduced as it is said that Archas came up

ORIGIN OF THE SPIRITUAL WORLD

heavy and very red. The material in Adoil may have gone through a process that caused them to become the hard Archas. The red color of Archas implies that it may have contained some particles or particle precursors which are not just like that of a simple light. The opening of Archas and its giving birth to the lowest things implies that something happened after Archas was split into different bodies. This also implies that the viscosity of Adoil and Archas were not strong enough to prevent them from dividing into other bodies. The dark color of some of the things that were born after Archas came apart suggests that Archas went through some processes that changed its original color from red to dark. The dark color can be the consequence of the types of matters present at that stage. The great and dark things that came out of Archas were then commanded to move and go below to become the foundation of the lowest things. A process may have been designed by God to allow the things that descended from Archas to move downward. That process may be related to how Archas was formed and how it has been shaped into different things. In other words, the movement of Archas from the position of Adoil, its precursor, to the lowest parts could have affected the state of the things that came out of it. According to the above story (2 Enoch 26), Archas moved until it stationed itself above the darkness and below that darkness, there was nothing else. The existence of darkness below also implies that the light that was created was not able to reach every part of the world, but it has some limits beyond which darkness ruled. In other words, at the lowest edge of the universe, there is darkness.

Seeing the motion of the most celestial bodies in the universe, it is likely that the movement of the remaining of Adoil that became Archas was not linear, but spiral or circular or something that turned. As it would have been the movement of Archas that communicated the initial movement to the celestial bodies in the universe.

To summarize what happened in 2 Enoch 25 and 26, at the command of God, Adoil was born. A great light was at the center or belly or in the middle of Adoil. God was at the center of that light. Then, God positioned his seat on His throne and commanded the created light to go above the throne. That light is the foundation of the things on high. In other words, the first stage of the formation of the universe was the formation of a huge body which inside was full of light. Then that body was fragmented to birth many pieces of body which are highly rich in light. After this stage, God commanded Adoil to harden and to split. Consequently, it hardened and became Archas. Archas was very heavy. God told Archas to go down and become the foundation of the lowest things, meaning that the things that came out of Adoil were moved to different places: some light went above the throne of God and the hard Archas went down and stationed above the darkness. Just as nothing was above the light above the throne of God, nothing was neither below the darkness below Archas. An empty space could have been between Archas and the throne of God. To put it in a different way, light was above

CHAPTER 3: FORMATION OF THE UNIVERSE ACCORDING TO THE HIDDEN SCRIPTURES

everything while darkness was below everything. "Adoil" is the product of the creation of physical things from nothing, "ex nihilo", whereas "Archas" was a formation of new things from the preexisting material of "Adoil". Between the darkness below and the light above was the space in which all things were created and formed. This suggests that the universe is not infinite but limited.

3.4. Formation of water and of the precursors of the Earth and the Sun

After Archas moved or as it was moving downward, it was split into many bodies. Consequently, more differentiations occurred, leading to the formation of the precursors of many bodies including the precursors of the Earth.

2 Enoch 27:1 And I commanded that there should be taken from light and darkness, and I said: Be thick, and it became thick, and I spread it out with the light, and it became water, and I spread it out over the darkness, below the light, and then I made firm the waters, that is to say the bottomless (abyss), and I made foundation of light around the water, and created seven circles from inside, and made the water look like crystal, wet and dry, so it was like glass, and the circles were around the waters and the other elements, and I showed each one of them its path, and the seven stars each one of them in its heaven, that they go the correct way, and I saw that it was good. 2 And I made separations between light and darkness in the midst of the water here and there, and I said to the light, that it should be the day, and to the darkness, that it should be the night, and there was evening and there was morning on the first day.

W. R. Morfill rendered the same story as:

2 Enoch 27:1 And I ordered that there should be a separation between the light and the darkness, and I said: 'Let there be a thick substance,' and it was so. 2. And I spread this out and there was water, and I spread it over the darkness, below the light. 3. And thus I made firm the waters, that is, the depths, and I surrounded the waters with light, and I created seven circles and I fashioned them like crystal, moist and dry, that is to say, like grass and ice, and as for the waters, and also the other elements, I showed each of them their paths, to the seven stars, each of them in their heaven, how they should go; and I saw that it was good. 4. And I separated between the light and the darkness; that is to say, between the waters here and there. And I said to the light: 'Let it be day'; and to the darkness, 'Let it be night'. And evening and the morning were the first day. (Translation by W.R. Morfill and edited by Henry Frowde).

The story in 2 Enoch 27 resembles that of the Genesis account by Moses. However, Moses did not say how water was formed. Because in the book of Genesis, the origin of water was not given, most people including even famous ministers think that God did not create water, but that it always existed. However, Enoch clearly explained the formation of water. But Enoch explained that water was formed after God spread its precursors, a thick substance, with light. Indeed, God commanded something to become thick, then He spread it over the darkness which is below the light. Some other translations (e.g. Joseph Limpkin) said that God spread those things with the light, suggesting that during the formation of the universe, light may have played a crucial role in stretching the universe. In other words, God may have used light to spread the precursors of the celestial bodies. This implies that during the formation of the universe, the energy of light was also used by God to move and spread things. Knowing the high speed and power of light, it may not have taken too long for it to stretch or expand the precursor of the universe and cause the precursors of celestial bodies to be positioned at specific places in the universe. Being one of the first things that God created, light could have played a crucial role during the formation and functioning of the universe. In my books *"Turbulent Origin of the Universe"* and *"Reconciling Science and Creation Accurately"*, I explained how the temperature of the precursors of celestial bodies and of the environment affected the processes that shaped them.

According to the law of physics applied to lever, a small force exerted over a greater distance can suffice to move a heavy weight. Light particles (e.g. photons) are small indeed, but their speed and the distance between celestial bodies could have allowed light to influence the motion of the precursors of celestial bodies and even the motion of celestial bodies today. Probably, the great distance between celestial bodies hides a code of how they were created and the forces involved in the spreading of their precursors! For instance, the Earth and the Sun may seem big, but when a force applied to them is located at a very far distance, it can easily move them just like a lever can significantly reduce the intensity of the force needed to move or lift things.

According to 2 Enoch 27, water was mixed with other elements, suggesting that the word "water" used in the Biblical and pseudepigraphic narratives of creation may not be taken literally as pure water (H_2O), but as water mixed with other chemical particles. The surrounding of water with light (2 Enoch 27:1) suggests that light must have pushed the waters from different angles and consequently contributed to mold them. It makes sense why God created light beforehand and then, used it to spread out things and much more.

The seven circles that God fashioned like crystal, moist and dry, may be the precursors of the seven stars mentioned in the same chapter (2 Enoch 27). According to Jewish literatures, the word used to refer to stars can mean any bright object in the sky, including planets. Therefore, stars here is referring to some celestial bodies. However, the surrounding of some waters by light may also mean that God covered the precursors of some celestial bodies with light, and/or that their interior may have been a substance different from light. It is also possible that some bodies like the Sun have water in their interior but are surrounded by a lot of light on their surface. 2 Enoch 27 also talked about some bodies like ice, which can be referred to as

CHAPTER 3: FORMATION OF THE UNIVERSE ACCORDING TO THE HIDDEN SCRIPTURES

some celestial bodies made of ice or covered with ice. The story clearly said that water was not the only element present at this point of the formation of the Earth, but other elements were formed by the end of the first day. Here, elements may not be referring to chemical elements or atoms only, but also to molecules and things even smaller than the current smallest subatomic particles. Furthermore, the story revealed that God showed the stars, ice, water, and other elements their paths. Path here can be the orbit of these bodies. Regardless of the size of the bodies and elements, their movements, speed, orbit, and trajectory were precisely defined by God.

Another Book by Nathanael-Israel Israel:
HOW GOD CREATED BABY UNIVERSE

THE FIRST AND ONLY BOOK THAT ACCURATELY EXPLAINS EVERYTHING ABOUT THE FORMATION OF THE UNIVERSE AND LIFE IN A WONDERFUL LANGUAGE THAT ALL CHILDREN AGES 7-12 CAN EASILY, FULLY UNDERSTAND & ENJOY!

As the only universe-origin book that your whole family will like and enjoy together, *"How God Created Baby Universe"* will set children on the path of success by accurately showing them early in life the formation of the universe, and how to detect errors in theories or stories that would misguide them as they grow up. Therefore, you need to add this great, efficient, trustworthy, and cost-effective book to the strategic journey of children toward their best tomorrow. With *"How God Created Baby Universe"*, you will:

- Have a peace of mind that children will get accurate, fit, and easy to understand universe-origin information that will produce real results in their life
- Become the leader that captures the heart of children craving for the original explanation of the formation of the universe so you can clear their way for freedom, power, technology, innovation, and breakthroughs of the future (learn more at Science180.com/children)
- Protect yourself and loved ones from wrong theories in the literature and the media by keeping children secured and empowered with the true knowledge of how the universe began
- Ultimately boost children's confidence in detecting, confronting, and avoiding wrong theories by knowing the facts and real processes involved in the formation of the universe

- Help children to easily sort out their origin-related questions using strategies that get them to tap into deep secrets that even highly educated people ignore
- Clearly explain to children how to mathematically know without a doubt whether God created the universe as the Bible says or billions of years evolution processes formed it
- Accurately explaining the complex formation of the universe and of life to children can be very hard in our modern world, but by getting *"How God Created Baby Universe"*, you will know the proven formula to help children to easily understand their huge universe-origin and life-origin questions with confidence, humor, and joy. They will surely laugh aloud while reading this book and thank you for it! It is time to buy this pragmatic book to help the children in your life today.

Member of the American Association for the Advancement of Science, American Chemical Society, and the American Society for Microbiology, **Dr. Nathanael-Israel Israel is** a Beninese-American scientist and international consultant, who shows the world how to scientifically decode the formation of the universe, of life, and who is known as the creator of the Chemicals Turbulent Origin Formula™, the inventor of the Life Turbulent Origin Formula™, and the discoverer of the Universe Creation Formula™. Learn more at Israel120.com.

Another Book by Nathanael-Israel Israel:
HOW BABY UNIVERSE WAS BORN

If you don't believe in God or you hate God, or you don't think there is anything or anyone called God, but you want your children to understand how the universe was formed from a scientifically-proven perspective that considers the facts, then this book is for your children.

Dr. Nathanael-Israel Israel is the founder of Science180, the American organization that helps people enter the realm of true knowledge about the universe formation. In other words, he is known as the first human being to ever use modern science to give people the state-of-the-art decoding experience of the origin of the universe and of life.

3.5. Formation of the Earth from large rocks that God piled up
The account in 2 Enoch 28 described how the precursor of the earth was

CHAPTER 3: FORMATION OF THE UNIVERSE ACCORDING TO THE HIDDEN SCRIPTURES

molded into the Earth:

2 Enoch 28:1 And then I made firm the heavenly circle and **made that the lower water which is under heaven collect itself together into one whole (piece), and that the chaos become dry, and it became so. 2 Out of the waves I created hard and large rock, and from the rock I piled up the dry (land), and the dry (land) I called earth, and the middle of the earth I called the abyss, or the bottomless.** *I collected the sea in one place and bound it together with a yoke. 3 And I said to the sea: Behold I give you eternal limits, and you shall not break loose from your integral parts. 4 Thus I made the firmament hold together. This day I called the first-created, Sunday.* (Translation by Joseph B. Lumpkin)

According to the translation by W.R. Morfill edited by Henry Frowde, the story read like this:

2 Enoch 28:1 And thus I made firm the circles of the heavens, and caused the waters below, which are under the heavens to be gathered into one place, and that the waves should be dried up, and it was so. 2. Out of the waves I made firm and great stones, and out of the stones, I heaped together a dry substance, and I called the dry substance earth. 3. And in the midst of the earth I appointed a pit, that is to say an abyss. 4. I gathered the sea into one place, and I restrained it with a yoke. And I said to the sea: 'Lo! I give thee an eternal portion and thou shalt not move from thy established position'. So, I made fast the firmament and fixed it above the water. 5. This I called the first day of the creation. Then it was evening, and again morning, and it was the second day. (Translation by W.R. Morfill and edited by Henry Frowde)

The statement "*I made firm the circles of the heavens*" implies that, after creating the precursors of celestial bodies, God may have applied some force to harden or make them firm. In other words, the hardening of the precursors of celestial bodies appeared after the precursors were formed. Similarly, for the earth to be formed, God gathered waters (not just H_2O) and dried it up to form rocks that He then piled together: "*I created hard and large rock, and from the rock I piled up the dry (land), and the dry (land) I called earth*".

The formation of rocks was finalized before the final shape of the Earth was given. This means that the rocks may have been glued or put together with a solution including the waters that was covering them. Consequently, we can deduce that if the rocks were not piled together, the earth could have been a cluster of rocks moving together like asteroids in the main belt! In other words, the inability to glue rocks together may explain why asteroids in the main belt are spread all over and move side by side.

After forming the dry land, God drained the water out of the land and then, barricaded it with eternal limits. According to 2 Enoch 28, there were many bodies of water before the formation of earth; and it was the lower waters under heaven or the waters below that were gathered together to form the earth. The other waters would have become other bodies, including celestial bodies. Some of those bodies of water were stored and may have been used to flood the Earth during the time of Noah. In other words, part of the water above and/or below the Earth could have been what was poured onto Earth during the Great Flood (Genesis 6:1-8).

Furthermore, 2 Enoch 47:5 also summarized how the earth was created:

2 Enoch 47:5 The Lord has placed the foundations in the unknown, and has spread out heavens, both physical and spiritual; he anchored the earth on the waters and created countless creatures. Who has counted the water and the foundation of the mutable (changeable, corruptible), or the dust of the earth, or the sand of the sea, or the drops of the rain, or the morning dew, or the wind's blowing (breathing)? Who has filled earth and sea, and the indestructible winter? 6 I (The Lord) cut the stars out of fire, and decorated heaven, and put it in their midst.

Although the story in Genesis 1 did not specify how the layers of fluids could have separated but just mentioned a separation of waters from waters, the Books of Enoch provided evidences for the separation and gathering together of precursors of bodies (2 Enoch 27-28). The creation narrative of the Book of Jubilees also agrees with the narrative in Genesis 1 that waters were separated on day 2 and beforehand, on day 1, God made the precursors of the things and laws which formed the celestial bodies and their characteristics. If you want to learn more about these mysteries, you will find the following books very useful:

- *"From Science to Bible's Conclusions"*
- *"Science180 Accurate Scientific Proof of God"*

You will highly benefit from checking them out.

3.6. Stars and celestial bodies were formed from a fire

According to Enoch, God formed stars from a fire:

2 Enoch 47: 1 [the Lord] cut the stars out of fire, and decorated heaven, and put it in their midst.

A look at the Sun should be enough to prove to anyone that it is made of fire. Knowing that in ancient documents, stars can mean anything shining in the sky, all celestial bodies could have been made from a fiery substance. Otherwise, what is the source of the energy in all matter? A difficult task can be how to demonstrate the way a fire or fiery substance was molded into the various things in nature. Another interesting question would be why some celestial bodies like stars still have fire, whereas other bodies like the earth has no fire at their surface, but in their interior as volcanic eruptions have proven. An interesting question would be, why some celestial bodies like the earth have lava in their interior and how that can be connected to the original fiery substance they descended from? I reviewed these mysteries in the following books:

- *"Turbulent Origin of the Universe"*
- *"Reconciling Science and Creation Accurately"*
- *"From Science to Bible's Conclusions"*

CHAPTER 3: FORMATION OF THE UNIVERSE ACCORDING TO THE HIDDEN SCRIPTURES

- *"Science180 Accurate Scientific Proof of God"*

Some Biblical references suggest that fire may be a primordial thing God used to create things, and it will likely be the product of everything after the universe is destroyed at the end times. For instance, while warning his followers about the coming of the Day of the Lord, Apostle Peter revealed how God will destroy the world by fire (2 Peter 3:1-18, Tree of Life version):

2 Peter 3:*1 Loved ones, this is now the second letter that I am writing to you. In both I am trying to stir you up by way of a reminder to wholesome thinking— 2 to remember the words previously proclaimed by the holy prophets and the commandment of our Lord and Savior through your emissaries. 3 First of all, understand that in the last days, scoffers will come scoffing, following after their own desires 4 and saying, "Where is this promise of His coming? Ever since the fathers died, everything goes on just as it has from the beginning of creation." 5 For in holding to this idea, it escapes their notice that* **the heavens existed long ago and the earth was formed out of water and through water by the word of God. 6 Through these, the world of that time was destroyed by being flooded with water. 7 But by the same word the present heavens and earth are being reserved for fire—kept until the Day of Judgment and the destruction of ungodly people. 8 But don't forget this one thing, loved ones, that with the Lord one day is like a thousand years, and a thousand years are like one day.** *9 The Lord is not slow in keeping His promise, as some consider slowness. Rather, He is being patient toward you—not wanting anyone to perish, but for all to come to repentance.* 10 **But the day of the Lord will come like a thief. On that day the heavens will pass away with a roar, and the elements will melt and disintegrate, and the earth and everything done on it shall be exposed.** *11 Since all these things are to be destroyed in this way, what kind of people should you be? Live your lives in holiness and godliness, 12 looking for and hastening the coming of the day of God.* **In that day the heavens will be dissolved by fire, and the elements will melt in the intense heat. 13 But in keeping with His promise, we look for new heavens and a new earth, where righteousness dwells.** *14 Therefore, loved ones, while you are looking for these things, make every effort to be found in shalom, spotless and blameless before Him. 15 Bear in mind that the patience of our Lord means salvation—just as our dearly loved brother Paul also wrote to you with the wisdom given to him. 16 He speaks about these matters in all of his letters.* **Some things in them are hard to understand, which the ignorant and unstable twist (as they also do with the rest of the Scriptures)—to their own destruction.** *17 Since you already know all this, loved ones, be on your guard so that you are not led astray by the error of the lawless and lose your sure footing. 18 Instead, keep growing in the grace and knowledge of our Lord and Savior Yeshua the Messiah. To Him be the glory both now and to the day of eternity! Amen.*

3.7. Formation of the Sun on the fourth day

Just like the Bible's Book of Genesis, the Books of Enoch also said that God formed the Sun on the fourth day:

2 Then came evening, and morning came of the fourth day. 3 On Wednesday, the fourth day, I commanded that there should be great lights on the heavenly circles. 4 On the first uppermost circle I placed the stars, Cronus, and on the second Aphrodite, on the third Ares, on the fifth Zeus, on the sixth Ermis (Hermes), on the seventh lesser the moon, and adorned it with the lesser stars. 5 And on the lower (parts) I placed the sun for the illumination of day, and the moon and stars for the illumination of night. 6 (And I set) the sun that it should go according to each of the twelve constellations, and I appointed the succession of the months and their names and lives, their thundering, and how they mark the hours, and how they should proceed. 7 Then evening came and morning came of the fifth day.

3.8. Formation of plants, animals, and man

After the completion of the formation of the Earth, God commanded it to produce plants. At this point, the story is very similar to that recounted in the Bible's Book of Genesis:

2 Enoch 30:1 **On the third day I commanded the earth to make and grow great and fruitful trees, and hills, and seeds to sow, and I planted Paradise, and enclosed it, and placed armed guards in the form of my flaming angels, and in this way, I created renewal...***8 On Thursday, the fifth day, I commanded the sea, that it should bring forth fishes, and feathered birds of many varieties, and all animals creeping over the earth, going forth over the earth on four legs, and soaring in the air, of male and female sex, and every soul breathing the spirit of life. 9 And there came evening, and there came morning of the sixth day. 10 On Friday, the sixth day, I commanded my wisdom to create man from seven consistent applications: one, his flesh from the earth; two, his blood from the dew; three, his eyes from the sun; four, his bones from stone; five, his intelligence from the swiftness of the angels and cloud; six, his veins and his hair from the grass of the earth; seven, his soul from my breath and from the wind. 11 And I gave him seven natures: to the flesh - hearing, the eyes for sight, to the soul - smell, the veins for touch, the blood for taste, the bones for endurance, to the intelligence - enjoyment. 12 I created a saying (speech) from knowing. I created man from spiritual and from physical nature, from both come his death and life and appearance. He knows speech like some created thing. He is small in greatness and great in smallness, and I placed him on earth, like a second angel, to be honorable, great and glorious. And I appointed him as ruler to rule on earth and to have my wisdom, and there was none like him on earth of all my existing creatures. 13 And I appointed him a name made from the four components, from east, from west, from south, and from north. And I appointed for him four special stars, and I called his name Adam, and showed him the two ways, the light and the darkness, and I told him: 14 This is good, and that bad, so that I should learn whether he has love towards me, or hatred, and so that it would be clear who in his race loves me. 15 For I have seen his nature, but he has not seen his own nature, and therefore by not seeing it he will sin worse, and I said, "After sin is there nothing but death?" 16 And I put sleep into him and he fell asleep. And I took from him a rib, and created a wife, so that death should come to him by his wife, and I took his last word and called her name mother, that is to say, Eve.*

CHAPTER 3: FORMATION OF THE UNIVERSE ACCORDING TO THE HIDDEN SCRIPTURES

Although the Bible did not specify when the Garden of Eden was planted on Earth, the Books of Enoch said that it was on the 3rd day, the same day that plants were formed. In an incoming chapter, I will talk about the life of the first human beings (Adam and Eve) in the Garden of Eden before and after they sinned.

3.9. God is the creator of all forces in the universe

Most things in the universe are interconnected and some of these interactions intervene via what people perceive as forces or fields. Most people vulgarly think that gravity is a force, but most scientists would say not. Regardless of the how people would define them, the forces, fields, or interactions in the universe have been created for specific reasons. The Books of Enoch stated God created all forces in the universe and they obeyed Him. These forces certainly include those holding together the small materials or particles as well as the big celestial bodies in the universe.

2 Enoch 33:8 **For I created all forces, and there is none that resists me and none that does not subject himself to me. For all subject themselves to my kingdom, and labor for my complete rule.**

3.10. God stretched heavens

Enoch mentioned that God stretched heaven (2 Enoch 47:5), confirming some 21st century scientific evidences according to which the universe is expanding:

2 Enoch 47:5 **The Lord has placed the foundations in the unknown, and has spread forth heavens visible (physical) and invisible (spiritual);** *He fixed the earth on the waters, and created countless creatures, and who has counted the water and the foundation of the unfixed, or the dust of the earth, or the sand of the sea, or the drops of the rain, or the morning dew, or the wind's breathings? Who has filled earth and sea, and the indissoluble winter? 6 I cut the stars out of fire, and decorated heaven, and put it in their midst.*

In the Bible, the stretching of the universe was also announced (e.g. Isaiah 42:5, Isaiah 45:12, Isaiah 48:13).

'Science180 Academy' Success Strategy:
SCIENCE180 SERVICES AND PRODUCTS YOU WILL LOVE

Because you are reading this book, you are probably very interested in answering your questions about the origin of the universe, of life, and of chemicals. Imagine you want to be trained by Dr. Nathanael-Israel Israel and his team so you can benefit from their outstanding expertise to empower yourself or your team. Or you want him to give a keynote speech, a seminar, or any other kind of talk or conference at your organization. Or you want him to mentor you or some people or team at your organization. Maybe you have critical origin-related questions that you need his help to accurately answer. You want a true expert to talk with you about the customized program or game plan that fits your needs. You want him to tailor his advice, expert feedback, and proven shortcuts to the stage of life you are in and help you get to where you want to be in your desire to properly understand the origin of the universe, life, and chemicals and harness the benefits that come with it. Perhaps you don't know how to properly get any of these important tasks done according to your specific needs or the needs and demands of your organization. That is what Science180 Academy is all about. Visit Science180.com/services for more details about how to benefit from the services that Science180 provides.

Maybe you are a leader that wants to hire Dr. Nathanael-Israel Israel and his team to train some departments at your organization. Or you want to refer them to other companies like a good dish passed around the dinner table, and you want to explore how Nathanael-Israel Israel can pay you something for that referral. Maybe you attended Nathanael-Israel Israel's speaking program, for which, without going into details, he accurately raised your awareness about how the universe, life, and chemicals were formed. Or maybe you attended his training, in which he detailed and showed you how he decoded the scientific data using various tools and certain thinking strategies that helped him and which transferred some skills to you; and now, you are interested in a long term one-on-one consulting, or mentoring program with him, so that, he delves into more details about how to use proven techniques to decode the universe (strategies for data collection, data analysis, data presentation, writing, and even tips for future research) and change your behavior on a long term basis. If you related to any of the points mentioned above, Science180 Academy is the right fit for you! Other customizable services that Science180 provides include: Assessments, Book publishing, Conferences, Consulting, Executive mastermind groups, Face-to-face visits, Master classes, Online courses, Podcasting, Seminars, Speaking engagements Video programs

CHAPTER 4

WHY DO PEOPLE IGNORE THIS INDISPUTABLE STORY ABOUT THE FORMATION OF ANGELS AND THEIR CONTROL OF CELESTIAL BODIES– YET THEIR LIFE DEPENDS ON IT EVEN IF THEY DON'T KNOW?

4.1. Date and process of the creation of angels
The Book of Jubilees recounts that on the first day of creation, God created many types of angels:
Jubilees 2:1 *And the angel of the face spoke to Moses by the command of the Lord, saying: " Write all the words of creation, how in six days the Lord God finished all the works which he created, and rested on the seventh day and sanctified it for all the years and established it as a sign for all his works."* **For on the first day he created the heavens above and the earth and the waters and all the spirits that serve before him, and the angels of the face and the angels- that cry "holy," and the angels of the spirit of fire, and the angels of the spirit of wind, and the angels of the spirit of the clouds of darkness and of hail and of hoarfrost, and the angels of the abysses and of thunder and of lightning, and the angels of the spirits of cold and of heat, of winter and of spring and of fall and of summer and of all the spirits of the multitude of works which are in the heavens and on the earth and in all the depths, and of darkness and of light and of dawn and of eve which he has prepared in the knowledge of his heart.** *2. And at that time we saw his work and praised him and lauded before him on account of all his work, for seven great things did he make on the first day. And on the second day he made a firmament between the waters, and the waters divided on this day, and half of it ascended upward, and half of it descended beneath the firmament over the face of the earth. And this work alone was made on the second day.* (Jubilees 2:1-3).

This story showed that many phenomena (e.g. fire, darkness, light, dawn,

ORIGIN OF THE SPIRITUAL WORLD

wind, clouds, hail, hoarfrost, thunder, lightning, cold, heat, winter, spring, fall, summer, and multitude of works in the universe) that some people may think are controlled by mere physical processes are in fact under the control of angels.

The second Book of Enoch explained how God made angels with fire which He cut from stones:

2 Enoch 29:1 And for all the heavenly hosts, I fashioned a nature like that of fire, and my eye gazed on the very firm and hard stone. And from the brightness of My eye the lightning received its wonderful nature. 2. And fire is in the water and water in the fire, and neither is the one quenched, nor the other dried up. On this account lightning is brighter than the Sun, and soft water is stronger than hard stone. 3. And from the stone I cut the mighty fire. And from the fire I made the ranks of the spiritual hosts, ten thousand angels, and their weapons are fiery, and their garment is a burning flame, and I ordered them to stand each in their ranks.

According to Joseph B. Lumpkin, the same chapter translates as:

2 Enoch 29:1 And for all the heavenly soldiers I made them the image and essence of fire, and my eye looked at the very hard, firm rock, and from the gleam of my eye the lightning received its wonderful nature, (which) is both fire in water and water in fire, and one does not put out the other, nor does the one dry up the other, therefore the lightning is brighter than the sun, softer than water and firmer than hard rock. 2 And from the rock I cut off a great fire, and from the fire I created the orders of the incorporeal (spiritual / non-physical) ten troops of angels, and their weapons are fiery and their raiment a burning flame, and I commanded that each one should stand in his order.

4.2. Angels control celestial bodies and natural phenomenon

Enoch learned about several angels during his visit to the heavens. The book on 3 Enoch particularly gives a very deep insight into the nature, works, ranks and organization of angels. Because my goal here is not to deeply study angels, I will not focus on them in this chapter. In other books, I detailed angels. Some of the most known angels are archangels (1 Enoch 20):

- Uriel is over the world, turmoil, and terror.
- Raphael is over the spirits of men.
- Raguel takes vengeance on the world of the luminaries.
- Michael is set over the virtues of humankind and over chaos.
- Saraqael is set over the spirits, who sin in the spirit.
- Gabriel is over Paradise and the serpents and the Cherubim.
- Remiel is set over those who rise.

In 3 Enoch 14-28, the name of some angels that controlled certain physical things in the universe were revealed.

As of today, some of those angels are under the control of Enoch; for Enoch was promoted by God after he was taken to heaven. Moreover, according to the first Book of Enoch, before being taken to heaven, Enoch

CHAPTER 4: FORMATION OF ANGELS AND THEIR CONTROL OF CELESTIAL BODIES

lived among angels somewhere on Earth. One of the transformations Enoch went through after being taken to heaven was the change of his body into fire and flames (3 Enoch 15).

3 Enoch 14:(3) And even the angel of fire, and the angel of hail, and the angel of wind, and the angel of the lightning, and the angel of wrath, and the angel of the thunder, and the angel of the snow, and the angel of the rain; and the angel of the day, and the angel of the night, and the angel of the sun, and the angel of the moon, and the angel of the planets, and the angel of the constellations whose hands rule the world, **all of them feared and shook and were frightened when they looked at me** [Enoch]. *(4) These are the names of the rulers of the world:* **Gabriel, the angel of fire**, *Baradi-el, the angel who controls hail, Ruchi-el who controls the wind,* **Baraqi-el who controls the lighting**, *Zahafi-el who controls the winds of the storm, Rahami-el who controls the thunders, Rahashi-el who controls the earthquake, Shalgiel who controls the snow, Matari-el who controls the rain,* **Shimshi-el who controls the planets, Rahati-el who controls the constellations.** *(5) And they all fell to the ground and bowed, when they saw me* [Enoch]. *And they were not able to look at me because of the majestic glory of the crown on my head.*

This account corroborates with the Bible which says that angels were made to serve man who was created in the image of God. Therefore, it makes sense that a human being like Enoch who was taken to heaven by God was raised above angels. Similarly, when Jesus Christ was taken to heaven, the Bible says that He is elevated above all angels. Below, I detailed angels who control certain portions of the universe (3 Enoch 14-28). Although it is difficult to know what part of the universe their description is referring to, the story at least points to the fact that the universe is controlled by invisible forces. Although the following paragraphs dealing with angels may sound boring to some people, they are worth reading to grasp the complexity of the dynamics of the physical and spiritual world.

Angels rule over celestial bodies with authority. Angels that control the universe are highly ranked and they yield to their superior according to their limits and power (3 Enoch 18-24). The angelic hierarchy can be one of the factors that maintain the universe in a perfect harmony. Therefore, it may be difficult to scientifically explain how angels affect celestial bodies. To have a better view of the organization of bodies in the universe and in heavens, a careful review of 3 Enoch 18-24 may be needed.

In the following sections, I will review several types of angels:
- The princes of the seven heavens, and of the sun, moon, planets, and constellations
- Ranks of angels established by the homage
- Wheels of the Merkaba (chariot) and RIKBIEL, their Prince
- Chayoth and Chayoth and their Price, CHAYYLIEL
- Cherubim and their Prince, KERUBIEL

ORIGIN OF THE SPIRITUAL WORLD

- Ophannim and their Prince, OPHPHANNIEL
- Seraphim and their Prince, *SERAPHIEL*
- RADWERIEL, the keeper of the Book of Records
- Irin and Qaddishin (Watchers and Holy Ones)

Knowing that some people are interested in knowing the agents behind some phenomena in the universe, this chapter will answer some of those questions, including which angels control which part of the universe.

4.3. The princes of the seven heavens and of the Sun, the Moon, the planets, and the constellations

3 Enoch 17:(1) The number of princes is seven. They are the great, beautiful, wonderful, honored, and revered ones. They are assigned over the seven heavens, and these are they: MIKAEL *(Michael),* GABRIEL, SHATQIEL, BAKARIEL, BADARIEL, PARCHRIEL. *(Some sources omit Parchriel and add Sidriel). (2) And every one of them is the prince of the host of one heaven. And each one of them is accompanied by 496,000 groups of ten-thousand ministering angels. (3)* MIKAEL *is the great prince assigned to ruler over the seventh heaven, the highest one, which is in the Araboth (highest heaven).* **Gabriel is the prince of the host assigned to rule over the sixth heaven** *which is in Makon.* SHATAQIEL *is the prince of the host assigned to rule over the fifth heaven which is in Makon.* SHAHAQIEL *is the prince of the host assigned to rule over the* **fourth heaven** *which is in Zebul.* BADARIEL *is the prince of the host assigned to rule over the third heaven which is in Shehaqim.* BARAKIEL *is the prince of the host assigned to rule over the second heaven which is in the height of Raqia (heaven).* PAZRIEL *is the prince of the host assigned to rule over the* **first heaven** *which is in Wilon (or Velum, as the first heaven is called), which is in Shamayim. (4) Under them in* **GALGALLIEL, the prince who is assigned as ruler over the orb (galgal) of the sun**, *and with him are 96 great and revered angels who moves the sun in Raqia (heaven) a distance of 365,000 parasangs each day. (5) Under them is* **OPHANNIEL, the prince who is set the globe (Ophan) of the moon.** *And with him are 88 (some have it as 68) angels who move the globe of the moon 354 thousand parasangs every night at the time when the moon stands in the East at its turning point. And the moon is situated in the East at its turning point in the fifteenth day of every month. (6) Under them is* **RAHATIEL, the prince who is appointed to rule over the constellations**. *He is accompanied by 72 great and revered angels. And why is he called RAHATIEL? Because he makes the stars run (marhit) in their orbits and courses, which is 339 thousand parasangs every night from the East to West, and from West to East. The Holy One, blessed be He, has made a tent for all of them, for the sun, the moon, the planets and the stars, and they travel in it at night from the West to the East. (7) Under them is* **KOKBIEL, the prince who is assigned to rule over all the planets.** *And with him are 365,000 groups of ten thousand ministering angels, great and revered ones who move the planets from city to city and from province to province in Raqia (the heaven) of heavens. (8) And ruling over them are seventy-two princes of nations (kingdoms) on high corresponding to the 72 nations of the world. And all of them are crowned with crowns of*

CHAPTER 4: FORMATION OF ANGELS AND THEIR CONTROL OF CELESTIAL BODIES

royalty and clothed in royal clothes and wrapped in royal robes. And all of them are riding on royal horses and holding royal scepters in their hands. In front of each of them when he is traveling in Raqia (heaven), royal servants are running with great glory and majesty just as on earth the Princes are traveling in chariots with horsemen and great armies and in glory and greatness with praise, song, and honor. (Translation Joseph B. Lumpkin).

By the way parasang is a historical unit of walking distance estimated to be about 4.8-5.6 kilometers, equivalent of 3-3.5 miles. Before I close this segment, I would like to address the meaning on Raqia (firmament/heavens) mentioned above. Indeed, in the above section and in others, the word "Raqia" (heaven) is used many times. The word heavens and firmament are used a lot in the Books of Enoch and even in the Bible when the creation of the universe is addressed. However, their meaning is not very clear and it is hard to find a contemporary word in this space age that properly defines them. Also used in Genesis 1:6-8, "Raquia" is a key Hebrew word which is translated "firmament" in the King James Version and "expanse" in most Hebrew dictionaries and modern translations.

Genesis 1:*6 And God said,* **let there be a firmament** *in the midst of the waters, and let it divide the waters from the waters. 7 And God made the* **firmament** *and divided the waters which were under the firmament from the waters which were above the* **firmament:** *and it was so. 8 And God called the* **firmament Heaven.** *And the evening and the morning were the second day.* (King James Version)

During my reading of the third Books of Enoch, I found an interesting commentary that I would like to address here (3 Enoch 4:7):

"*Raqa means to spread out, beat out, or hammer as one would a malleable metal. It can also mean "plate." The Greek Septuagint translated raqia 16 out of 17 times with the Greek word stereoma, which means "a firm or solid structure." The Latin Vulgate (A.D. 382) used the Latin term "firmamentum" which also denotes solidness and firmness. The King James translators coined the word "firmament" because there was no single word equivalent in English. Today, "firmament" is usually used poetically to mean sky, atmosphere, or heavens. In Modern Hebrew, raqia means sky or heavens. However, originally it probably meant something solid or firm that was spread out.* (Translation by Joseph B. Lumpkin).

4.4. Ranks of angels established by the homage

3 Enoch 18:1 THE ANGELS OF THE FIRST HEAVEN, when (ever) they see their prince, they dismount from their horses and bow themselves. And THE PRINCE OF THE FIRST HEAVEN, when he sees the prince of the second heaven, he dismounts, removes the glorious crown from his head and bows himself to the ground. AND THE PRINCE OF THE SECOND HEAVEN, when he sees the prince of the third heaven, he removes the glorious crown from his head and bows himself to the ground. AND THE PRINCE OF THE THIRD HEAVEN, when he sees the prince of the fourth heaven, he removes the glorious crown from his head and bows himself to the ground. AND THE PRINCE OF THE FOURTH HEAVEN, when he sees

ORIGIN OF THE SPIRITUAL WORLD

the prince of the fifth heaven, he removes the glorious crown from his head and bows himself to the ground. AND THE PRINCE OF THE FIFTH HEAVEN, *when he sees the prince of the sixth heaven, he removes the glorious crown from his head and bows himself to the ground.* AND THE PRINCE OF THE SIXTH HEAVEN, *when he sees the prince of the seventh heaven, he removes the glorious crown from his head and bows himself to the ground.* (2) AND THE PRINCE OF THE SEVENTH HEAVEN, *when he sees* THE SEVENTY-TWO PRINCES OF KINGDOMS, *he removes the glorious crown from his head and bows himself to the ground.* (3) *And the seventy-two princes of kingdoms, when they see the door keepers of the first hall in the* ARABOTH RAQIA *in the highest heaven, they remove the royal crown from their head and bow themselves. And the door keepers of the first hall, when they see the doorkeepers of the second Hall, they remove the glorious crown from their head and bow themselves. The door keepers of the second hall, when they see the door keepers of the third hall, they remove the glorious crown from their head and bow themselves. The door keepers of the third hall, when they see the door keepers of the fourth hall, they remove the crown from their head and bow themselves. The door keepers of the fourth hall, when they see the door keepers of the fifth Hall, they remove the glorious crown from their head and bow themselves. The door keepers of the fifth hall, when they see the doorkeepers of the sixth hall, they remove the crown from their head and fall to their face. The door keepers of the sixth hall, when they see the door keepers of the seventh hall, they remove the glorious crown from their head and bow themselves.* (4) *And the door keepers of the seventh hall, when they see* The Four Great Princes, *the honored ones, who are appointed over the four Camps of* SHEKINA, *they remove the crowns of glory from their head and bow themselves.* (5) *And the four-great princes, when they see* TAGHAS, *the prince, great and honored with song (and) praise, at the head of all the children of heaven, they remove the glorious crown from their head and bow themselves.* (6) *And Taghas, the great and honored prince, when he sees* BARATTIEL, *the great prince of three fingers in the height of Araboth, the highest heaven, he removes the glorious crown from his head and bows himself to the ground.* (7) *And Barattiel, the great prince, when he sees* HAMON, *the great prince, the fearful and honored, beautiful and terrible, he who makes all the children of heaven to shake, when the time draws near that is set for the saying of the 'Thrice Holy', he removes the glorious crown from his head and bows himself to the ground. For it is written (Isa. 33:3): " At noise of the confusion at the anxious preparation of the salutation of "Holy, Holy, Holy" the people are fled; at the lifting up of yourself the nations are scattered,"* (8) *And Hamon, the great prince, when he sees* TUTRESSIEL, *the great prince he removes the glorious crown from his head and bows himself to the ground.* (9) *And Tutresiel YHWH, the great prince, when he sees* ATRUGIEL, *the great prince, he removes the glorious crown from his head and bows himself to the ground.* (10) *And Aatrugiel the great prince, when he sees* NA' ARIRIEL YHWH, *the great prince, he removes the glorious crown from his head and bows himself to the ground.* (11) *And Na'aririel YHWH, the great prince when he sees* SAANIGIEL, *the great prince, he removes the glorious crown from his head and bows himself to the ground.* (12) *And Sasnigiel YHWH, when he sees* ZAZRIEL YHWH, *the great prince, he removes the glorious crown from his head and bows himself to the*

CHAPTER 4: FORMATION OF ANGELS AND THEIR CONTROL OF CELESTIAL BODIES

ground. (13) And Zazriel YHWH, the prince, when he sees GEBURATIEL YHWH, the prince, he removes the glorious crown from his head and bows himself to the ground. (14) And Geburatiel YHWH, the prince, when he sees ARAPHIEL YHWH, the prince, he removes the glorious crown from his head and bows himself to the ground. (15) And Araphiel YHWH, the prince, when he sees ASHRUYLU, the prince, who presides in all the sessions of the children of heaven, he removes the glorious crown from his head and bows himself to the ground. (16) And Ashruylu YHWH, the prince, when he sees GALLISUR YHWH, THE PRINCE, WHO REVEALS ALL THE SECRETS OF THE LAW (Torah), he removes the glorious crown from his head and bows himself to the ground. (17) And Gallisur YHWH, the prince, when he sees ZAKZAKIEL YHWH, the prince who is appointed to write down the merits of Israel on the Throne of Glory, he removes the glorious crown from his head and bows himself to the ground. (18) And Zakzakiel YHWH, the great prince, when he sees ANAPHIEL YHWH, the prince who keeps the keys of the heavenly Halls, he removes the glorious crown from his head and bows himself to the ground. Why is he called by the name of Anaphiel? Because the shoulders of his honor and majesty and his crown and his splendor and his brilliance overshadow all the chambers of Araboth (highest heaven) of Raqia (heaven) on high even as the Maker of the World overshadows them. Regarding the Maker of the world, it is written that His glory covered the heavens, and the earth was full of His praise. The honor and majesty of Anaphiel cover all the glories of Araboth (highest heaven) the highest. (19) And when he sees SOTHER ASHIEL YHWH, the prince, the great, fearful and honored one, he removes the glorious crown from his head and bows himself to the ground. Why is he called Sother Ashiel? Because he is assigned to rule over the four heads of the river of fire, which are beside the Throne of Glory; and every single prince who goes out or enters before the Shekina, goes out or enters only by his permission. For the seals of the river of fire are entrusted to him. And furthermore, his height is 7000 groups of ten-thousand parasangs. And he stirs up the fire of the river; and he goes out and enters before the Shekina to expound what is recorded concerning the inhabitants of the world. According for it is written (Dan. 7:10): "the judgment was set, and the books were opened." (20) And Sother Ashiel the prince, when he sees SHOQED CHOZI, the great prince, the mighty, terrible and honored one, he removes the glorious crown from his head and falls upon his face. And why is he called Shoqed Chozi? Because he weighs all the merits of man on a scale in the presence of the Holy One, blessed be He. (21) And when he sees ZEHANPURYU YHWH, the great prince, the mighty and terrible one, honored, glorified and feared in the entire heavenly household, he removes the glorious crown from his head and bows himself to the ground. Why is he called Zehanpuryu? Because he commands the river of fire and pushes it back to its place. (22) And when he sees AZBUGA YHWH, the great prince, glorified, revered, honored, adorned, wonderful, exalted, loved and feared among all the great princes who know the mystery of the Throne of Glory, he removes the glorious crown from his head and bows himself to the ground. Why is he called Azbuga? Because in the future he will clothe the righteous and pious of the world with garments of life and wrap them in the cloak of life, so that they can live an eternal life in them. (23) And when he sees the two great princes, the strong one and the glorified one who *are standing above him, he removes the glorious crown from his head and bows himself to the ground. And these are the names of the two princes: SOPHERIEL YHWH (Sopheriel YHWH the Killer), the great prince, the honored, glorified, blameless, venerable, ancient and mighty one. (24) Why is he called Sopheriel YHWH who kills (Sopheriel YHWH the Killer)? Because he is assigned to control the books of the dead, so that everyone, when the day of his death draws near, is written by him in the books of the dead. Why is he called Sopheriel YHWH who makes alive (Sopheriel YHWH the Lifegiver)? Because he is assigned control over the books of life, so that everyone whom the Holy One, blessed be He, will bring into life, he writes him in the book of life, by authority of The Divine Majesty. Perhaps he might say: "Since the Holy One, blessed be He, is sitting on a throne, they are also sitting when writing." The Scripture teaches us (I Kings 22:19, 2 Chron. 28:18): "And all the host of heaven are standing by him." They are called "The host of heaven" in order to show us that even the Great Princes and all like them in the high heavens, fulfill the requests of the Shekina in no other way than standing. But how is it possible that they are able to write, when they are standing? (25) It is done thusly.*

4.5. Wheels of the Merkaba (chariot) and Rikbiel, their Prince; Chayoth and CHAYYLIEL, their prince

Talking about the Wheels of the Merkaba (chariot) and Rikbiel, their Prince, Enoch said:

3 Enoch 19:1 Above these three angels, who are these great princes, there is one Prince, distinguished, revered, noble, glorified, adorned, fearful, fearless, mighty, great, uplifted, glorious, crowned, wonderful, exalted, blameless, loved, like a ruler, he is high and lofty, ancient and mighty, there is none among the princes like him. His name is RIKBIEL YHWH, the great and revered prince who is standing by Merkaba (chariot). (2) And why is he called RIKBIEL? Because he is assigned to rule over the wheels of the Merkaba (chariot), and they are given to his authority.

Addressing the Chayoth and CHAYYLIEL, their prince, Enoch said:

3 Enoch 20:1 Above these [Chayoth] there is one great and mighty prince. His name is CHAYYLIEL YHWH, a noble and honorable prince, a prince before whom all the children of heaven tremble, a prince who is able to swallow up the entire earth in one moment at a single mouthful. (2) And why is he called CHAYYLIEL YHWH? Because he is assigned to rule over the Holy Chayoth and he strikes the Chayoth with lashes of fire: and glorifies them, when they give praise and glory and rejoicing and he causes them to hurry and say "Holy" "Blessed be the Glory of YHWH from His place!" (The Kedushah Sacred Salutation of Holy, Holy, Holy).

3 Enoch 21: (1) The Four Chayoth correspond to the four winds. Each Chayya is as big as the space of the entire world. And each one has four faces; and each face is like the face of the East (sunrise). (2) Each one has four wings and each wing is like the tent (ceiling) of the universe. (3) And each one has faces in the middle of faces and wings in the middle of wings. The size of the faces is 248 faces, and the size of the wings is 365 wings. (4) And everyone is crowned with 2000 crowns on his head. And each crown is

CHAPTER 4: FORMATION OF ANGELS AND THEIR CONTROL OF CELESTIAL BODIES

like the rainbow in the cloud. And its splendor is like the magnificence of the circle of the sun. And the sparks that go out from everyone are like the glory of the morning star (planet Venus) in the East.

4.6. Cherubim and KERUBIEL, their Prince

To my knowledge, no any other book has described angels and particularly the Cherubim as the Hebrew Book of Enoch. Without much comment, I will present below what Enoch revealed about them:

3 Enoch 22:1 Above these [Cherubim] *there is one prince, noble, wonderful, strong, and praised with all kinds of praise. His name is CHERUBIEL YHWH, a mighty prince, full of power and strength, a prince of highness, and Highness (is) with him, a righteous Prince, and Righteousness (is) with him, a holy prince, and holiness (is) with him, a prince of glorified in (by) thousand host, exalted by ten thousand armies (2)* **At his anger the earth trembles, at his anger the camps (of armies) are moved, from fear of him the foundations are shaken, at his chastisement the Araboth (highest heaven) trembles. (3) His stature is full of (burning) coals. The height is that of the seven heavens and the breadth of his stature is like the sea. (4) The opening of his mouth is like a lamp of fire. His tongue is a consuming fire. His eyebrows are like the splendor of the lightning. His eyes are like sparks of bright light. His face is like a burning fire. (5)** *And there is a crown of holiness upon his head on which the Explicit Name is graven, and lightning proceeds from it. And the bow of the Shekina is between his shoulders. And his sword is like lightning; and on his thighs there are arrows like flames, and upon his armor and shield there is a consuming fire, and on his neck there are coals of burning juniper wood and (also) around him (there are coals of burning juniper). ... (10) And the two princes of the Merkaba (chariot) are together with him. (11) Why is he called CHERUBIEL YHWH, the Prince? Because he is assigned to rule over the chariot of the Cherubim. And the mighty Cherubim are subject to his authority. ... (13) And the Cherubim are standing by the Holy Chayoth, and their wings are raised up to their heads (are as the height of their heads) and Shekina is (resting) upon them and the bright Glory is upon their faces and songs of praise are in their mouth and their hands are under their wings and their feet are covered by their wings and horns of glory are upon their heads and the splendor of Shekina on their face and Shekina is resting on them and sapphire stones surround them and columns of fire are on their four sides and columns of burning staves are beside them. (14) There is one sapphire on one side and another sapphire on the other side and under the sapphires there are coals of burning juniper wood. (15) And a Cherub is standing in each direction but the wings of the Cherubim surround each other above their heads in glory; and they spread them to sing with them a song to him that inhabits the clouds and to praise the fearful majesty of the king of kings with their wings. (16) And CHERUBIEL YHWH, is the prince who is assigned to rule over them. He arrays them in proper, beautiful and pleasant orders and he exalts them in all manner of exaltation, dignity and glory. And he hurries them in glory and might to do the will of their Creator every moment. Above their high heads continually dwells the glory of the high king "who dwells on the Cherubim."*

ORIGIN OF THE SPIRITUAL WORLD

As I tried to learn more about the juniper wood mentioned in verse 14 above, I noticed that it requires full sunlight. When they don't get enough sun, the branches spread apart in an effort to let more sunlight in and their damage can't be repaired. When burning, juniper wood gives off very minimal visible smoke, and the smoke is very aromatic. In ancient history, it was used for the ritual purification of temples and the spring-time cleansing and casting out of witchcraft or evil spirits. It is interesting that the Cherubim were using their wings to glorify God when the juniper wood is being burned.

3 Enoch 22 gave some astounding details about the distance separating the location of some angels in heaven. The length unit called parasang that you will see over and over in the following paragraphs is an ancient walking unit equivalent to about 3 to 3.5 miles, meaning about 4.8 to 5.6 km. The next story hints at how huge some angels are. However, because most human being ignore the position of those angels, it is hard to fully understand the content of the story just by using modern physical means. However, to give a full account of the dynamics of the bodies in the universe, one may need to be aware of the diversity of the spiritual beings present in the world and how they interact with one another.

3 Enoch 22-B 1 How are the angels standing on high? He said: A bridge is placed from the beginning of the doorway to the end, like a bridge that is placed over a river for everyone to pass over it. And three ministering angels surround it and sing a song before YHWH, the God of Israel. And standing before it are the lords of dread and captains of fear, numbering a thousand times thousand and ten thousand times ten thousand, and they sing praises and hymns before YHWH, the God of Israel. (3) Many bridges are there. There are bridges of fire and many bridges of hail. Also, many rivers of hail, numerous storehouses of snow, and many wheels of fire. (4) And how many are the ministering angels are there? 12,000 times ten-thousand: six-thousand time ten-thousand above and six (thousand times ten-thousand) below. And 12,000 are the storehouses of snow, six above and six below. And 24 times ten-thousand wheels of fire, 12 times ten-thousand above and 12 times ten-thousand below. And they surround the bridges and the rivers of fire and the rivers of hail. And there are numerous ministering angels, forming entries, for all the creatures that are standing in the midst thereof, over against the paths of Raqia (heaven) Shamayim. (5) What does YHWH, the God of Israel, the King of Glory do? The Great and Fearful God, mighty in strength, covers His face. (6) In Araboth (highest heaven) are 660,000 times ten-thousand angels of glory standing over against the Throne of Glory and the divisions of flaming fire. And the King of Glory covers His face; for else the Araboth (highest heaven) of Raqia (heaven) would be torn apart from its center because of the majesty, splendor, beauty, radiance, loveliness, brilliancy, brightness, and Excellency of the appearance of (the Holy One,) blessed be He. (7) There are innumerable ministering angels carrying out his will, many kings and princes in the Araboth (highest heaven) of His delight. They are angels who are revered among the rulers in heaven, distinguished, adorned with song and they bring love to the minds of those who are frightened by the splendor of Shekina, and their eyes are dazzled by the shining beauty of their King, their faces grow

CHAPTER 4: FORMATION OF ANGELS AND THEIR CONTROL OF CELESTIAL BODIES

black and their strength fails. (8) There are rivers of joy, streams of gladness, rivers of happiness, streams of victory, rivers of life, streams of friendship and they flow over and go out from in front of the Throne of Glory and grow large and wend their way through the gates on the paths to Araboth (highest heaven) of Raqia (heaven) at the voice of shouting and music of the CHAYYOTH, at the voice of the rejoicing of the cymbals of his OPHANNIM and at the melody of the cymbals of His Cherubim. And they grow great and go out with noise and with the sound of the hymn: "HOLY, HOLY, HOLY, IS THE LORD OF HOST; THE WHOLE EARTH IS FULL OF HIS GLORY!"

***3 Enoch 22 -C** (1) What is the distance between one bridge and another? Tens of thousands of parasangs. They rise up tens of thousands of parasangs, and they go down tens of thousands of parasangs. (2) The distance between the rivers of dread and the rivers of fear is 22 times ten-thousand parasangs; between the rivers of hail and the rivers of darkness 36 times ten-thousand parasangs; between the chambers of lightnings and the clouds of compassion 42 times ten-thousand parasangs; between the clouds of compassion and the Merkaba (chariot) 84 times ten thousand parasangs; between the Merkaba (chariot) and the Cherubim 148 times ten-thousand parasangs; between the Cherubim and the Ophannim 24 times ten-thousand parasangs; between the chambers of chambers and the Holy Chayoth 40,000 times ten-thousand parasangs; between one wing (of the Chayoth) and another 12 times ten-thousand parasangs; and the breadth of each one wing is of that same measure; and the distance between the Holy Chayoth and the Throne of Glory is 30,000 times ten-thousand parasangs. (3) And from the foot of the Throne to the seat there are 40,000 times ten-thousand parasangs. And the name of Him that sits on it: let the name be sanctified! (4) And the arches of the Bow are set above the Araboth (highest heaven), and they are 1000 thousands and 10,000 times ten thousand of parasangs high. Their measure is after the measure of the 'Irin and Qaddishin (the Watchers and the Holy Ones). As it is written, (Genesis 9:13) "My bow I have set in the cloud." It is not written here "I will set" but "I have set," that is to say; I have already set it in the clouds that surround the Throne of Glory. As His clouds pass by, the angels of hail turn into burning coal. (5) And a voice of fire goes down from the Holy Chayoth. And because of the breath of that voice they run (Ezekiel 1:14) to another place, fearing that it could command them to go; and they return for fear that it may injure them from the other side. Therefore "they run and return." (6) And these arches of the Bow are more beautiful and radiant than the radiance of the sun during the summer solstice. And they are brighter (whiter) than a flaming fire and they are large and beautiful. (7) Above the arches of the Bow are the wheels of the Ophannim. Their height is 1000 thousand and 10,000 times 10,000 units of measure after the measure of the Seraphim and the Troops (Gedudim).*

The millions of people on earth are likely nothing compared to the number of angels in the world. Yet, God knows them and each of us by name. He also knows the number of hairs on our head and even the number of the countless stars in the universe. Finally, before I move to the next type of angel, I need to underline that, before his fall, Lucifer (today called Satan or the Devil) used to be a cherub; in fact he was an anointed cherub (Ezekiel

28:14).

4.7. Ophannim and Ophphanniel, their Prince

3 Enoch 25:1 Above these [Ophannim], *there is one great prince, highly honored, fit to rule, fearful, ancient, and powerful. OPHAPHANNIEL YHWH is his name. (2) He has sixteen faces, four faces on each side, also a hundred wings on each side. And he has 8466 eyes, corresponding to the days of the year and sixteen on each side. (Other sources have it as: corresponding to the hours in a year.) (3) And in those two eyes of his face, in each one of them lightning is flashing, and from each one of them burning staves are burning; and no creature is able to look at them: for anyone who looks at them is burned up instantly. (4) His height is the distance of 2500 years' journey. No eye can see and no mouth can tell of the mighty power of his strength except the King of kings, the Holy One, blessed be He. He alone can tell. (5)* **Why is he called OPHPHANNIEL? Because he rules over the Ophannim and the Ophannim are given over to his authority.** *He stands every day and attends to them and makes them beautiful. And he raises them up and determines their activity. He polishes the place where they stand and makes their dwelling place bright. He even makes the corners of their crowns and their seats spotless. And he waits upon them early and late, by day and by night, in order to increase their beauty and make their dignity grow. He keeps them diligent in the praise of their Creator. (6) And all the Ophannim are full of eyes, and they are full of brightness; seventy-two sapphires are fastened to their garments on their right side and seventy-two sapphires are fastened to their garments on their left side. (7) And four carbuncle stones are fastened to the crown of every single one, the splendor of which shines out in the four directions of Araboth (the highest heaven) even as the splendor of the orb of the sun shines out in all the directions of the universe. And why is it called Carbuncle (Bare' qet)? Because its splendor is like the appearance of a lightning (Baraq). And tents of splendor, tents of brilliance, tents of brightness as of sapphire and carbuncle enclose them because of the shining appearance of their eyes.*

By the way, carbuncle stones mentioned in verse 7 above are currently ranked as the 5th most precious stone and they have healing properties.

4.8. Seraphim and their Prince, *SERAPHIEL*

3 Enoch 26 (1) Over them [Seraphim] *there is one prince, who is wonderful, noble, of great honor, powerful and terrible, a chief leader and a fast scribe. He is glorified, honored and loved. (2) He is completely filled with splendor, and full of praise. He shines and he is totally full of the brightness of light and beauty. He is full of goodness and greatness. (3) His face is identical to that of angels, but his body is like an eagle's body. (4) His is magnificent like lightning, his appearance like burning staves. His beauty like sparks. His honor burns bright like glowing coal. His majesty like chashmals, His radiance like the light of the planet Venus. His image is like the Sun. His height is as high as the seven heavens. The light from his eyebrows is seven times as bright. (5) The sapphire on his head is as large as the entire universe and as splendid as the great heavens in radiance. (6) His body is full of eyes like the stars of the sky, innumerable and cannot be known. Every eye is*

CHAPTER 4: FORMATION OF ANGELS AND THEIR CONTROL OF CELESTIAL BODIES

like the planet Venus. But there are some of them like the Moon and some of them like the Sun. From His ankles to his knees they are like stars twinkling (of lightning). From his knees to his thighs is like the planet Venus, across his thighs like the moon, from his thighs to his neck is like the sun. From his neck to his head is like the Eternal Light. (7) The crown on his head is like the splendor of the Throne of Glory. The size of the crown is the distance of 502 years' journey. There is no kind of splendor, no kind of brilliance, no kind of radiance, no kind of light in the universe that is not affixed to the crown. (8) The name of that prince is SERAPHIEL YHWH. And the crown on his head, its name is "the Prince of Peace." **And why is he called by the name of SERAPHIEL YHWH? Because he is assigned to rule over the Seraphim.** *And the flaming Seraphim are under his authority. And he presides over them by day and night and teaches them to sing, praise, and proclaim the beauty, power and majesty of their King. They proclaim the beauty of their King through all types of Praise and Sanctification. (Kedushah - Sacred Salutation of Holy, Holy, Holy). (9)* **How many Seraphim are there? Four, equating to the four winds of the world. And how many wings have each one of them? Six, relating to the six days of Creation. And how many faces do they have? Each one of them have four faces. (10) The height measurement of the Seraphim is the height of the seven heavens. The size of each wing is like the span of all Raqia (heaven). The size of each face is like the face of the East. (11) And each one of them gives out light, adding to the splendor of the Throne of Glory, so that not even the Holy Chayoth, the honored Ophannim, nor the majestic Cherubim are able to look on it. Anyone who gazes at it would be blinded because of its great splendor. (12) Why are they called Seraphim? Because they burn (saraph) the writing tables of Satan: Every day Satan sits together with SAMMAEL, the Prince of Rome, and with DUBBIEL, the Prince of Persia, and they write down the sins of Israel on their writing tables, which they hand over to the Seraphim, so that the Seraphim can present them to the Holy One, blessed be He, so that He should eliminate (destroy) Israel from the world. But the Seraphim know the secrets of the Holy One, blessed be He. They know that He does not want the people Israel to perish. What do the Seraphim do about this? Every day they receive the tablets from the hand of Satan and they burn them in the burning fire, which is near the high and exalted Throne. They do this in order that the tablet should not come before the Holy One, blessed be He, when he is sitting upon the Throne of Judgment, judging the entire world in truth.**

4.9. RADWERIEL, the keeper of the Book of Records

3 Enoch 27 (1) Above the Seraphim there is one prince, exalted above all princes. He is more wonderful than all the servants. His name is **RADWERIEL YHWH who is assigned to rule over the treasuries of the books. (2) He couriers the Case of Writings, which has the Books of Records in it, and he brings it to the Holy One, blessed be He. And he breaks the seals of the case, opens it, and takes**

ORIGIN OF THE SPIRITUAL WORLD

out the books and delivers them before the Holy One, blessed be He. And the Holy One, blessed be He, receives them out of his hand and gives them to the Scribes to see so they may read them in the Great Beth (house) Din in the height of Araboth (highest heaven) of Raqia (heaven), before the household of heaven. (3) **And why is he called RADWERIEL? Because from every word going out of his mouth an angel is created.** He stands in the service of the company of the ministering angels and sings a song before the Holy One, blessed be He, as the time draws near for the recitation of the Thrice Holy One.

4.10. Irin and Qaddishin (Watchers and Holy Ones)

3 Enoch 28 (1) *Above all these there are four great princes. Their names are Irin and Qaddishin. They are highly honored, revered, loved, wonderfully glorious, and greater than any of the heavenly children. There is none like them among all the princes of heaven (sky).* **There are none equal to them among any Servants. Each one is equal to all the rest of the heavenly servants put together. (2) And their dwelling is near the Throne of Glory and their standing place near the Holy One, blessed be He. The brightness of their dwelling is a reflection from the brightness from the Throne of Glory. Their face is magnificent and is a reflection of the magnificence of Shekina. (3) They are elevated by the glory of the Divine Majesty (Gebura) and praised by (through) the praise of Shekina. (4) And not only that, but the Holy One, blessed be He, does nothing in his world without first consulting them. Only after He consults them does He perform it.** *As it is written (Daniel 4: 17): "The sentence is by the decree of the Irin and the demand by the word of the Qaddishin." (5)* **The Irin are two (twins) and the Qaddishin are two (twins)**. *In what fashions standing before the Holy One, blessed be He? We should understand that* **one Ir is standing on one side and the other Ir on the other side. Also, one Qaddish is standing on one side and the other on the other side.** *(6) And they exalt the humble forever, and they humble and bring to the ground those that are proud. They exalt to the heights those that are humble. (7) And every day, as the Holy One, blessed be He, is sitting upon the Throne of Judgment and judges the entire world, and the Books of the Living and the Books of the Dead are opened in front of Him all the children of heaven are standing before Him in fear and dread. They are in awe and they shake.* **When the Holy One, blessed be He, is sitting on the Throne of Judgment to execute His judgment, His garment is white as snow, the hair on his head is like pure wool and His entire cloak is shining with light. He is covered with righteousness all over, like He is wearing a coat of mail. (8) And those Irin and Qaddishin (Watchers and Holy Ones) are standing before Him like court officers before the judge.** *And constantly they begin and argue a case and close the case that comes before the Holy One, blessed be He, in judgment, according for it is written (Daniel 4. 17): "The sentence is by the decree of the Irin and the demand by the word of Qaddishin." (9) Some of them argue the case and others pass the sentence in the Great Beth Din (Great House of the Sanhedrin) in Araboth (the highest heaven). Some of them make requests in the presence of the Divine*

CHAPTER 4: FORMATION OF ANGELS AND THEIR CONTROL OF CELESTIAL BODIES

Majesty and some close the cases before the Most High. Others finish by going down and confirming the judgment and executing the sentences on earth below. According for it is written (Daniel 4. 13, 14): "Behold an Ir and a Qaddish came down from heaven and cried aloud and said, "Chop down the tree, and cut off his branches, shake off his leaves, and scatter his fruit: let the beasts escape from under it, and the fowls from his branches." **(10) Why are they called Irin and Qaddishin (Watchers and Holy Ones)? Because they sanctify the body and the spirit with beatings with fire on the third day of the judgment, for it is written (Hosea 6: 2): "After two days will he revive us: on the third he will raise us up, and we shall live before him."**

According to Joseph B. Lumpkin, *"Irin and Qaddishin are two pairs of angels forming the apex of angelic power"*. In other words, no other angel is higher than them. It is impossible for any human being to explain the dynamics of the universe without referring to the complex nature, ranks, works, and mission of angels. Heaven did not create the universe, but God did. However, after creation, God has been involving angels in its dynamics, maintenance, and functioning of its inhabitants (nonliving things and living organisms).

'Science180 Academy' Success Strategy:
SCIENCE180 ACADEMY PROGRAMS

Owned by Science180, Science180 Academy is a training, speaking, consulting, and mentoring program specialized in everything universe-origin, life-origin, chemicals-origin, and anything at the intersection of reason and faith, or science and religion.

Science180 Academy deals with different subjects according to the needs of its members or target groups. When people register to Science180 Academy, they must choose the program(s) they want to focus on so their training can be properly personalized accordingly. This is similar to how people register to a university, and take classes in a specific department matching their needs!

Science180's breakthroughs are so complex and dense that it is not realistic or good to try to explain all in just one academy, else people will be overwhelmed, disinterested, and confused by the plethora of data to handle. In other words, Science180 Academy offers a wide range of origin-related training in various domains strategically designed to allow people to choose the most suitable for their needs so that, regardless of their background or field of expertise, people can equip themselves, align their mindset, improve lives today and forever using the accurate explanation of the origin of the universe, of life, and of chemicals. Science180 Academy curriculum is based on 12 years of deep unconventional research that culminated with the publication of many much-admired books on the formation of the universe and its content: See www.Science180.com/books

The content of each Science180 Academy is strategically crafted by Dr. Nathanael-Israel Israel (who is acknowledged as the internationally-acclaimed world's authority in origin-related issues) to suit both scientists and nonscientists, religious and nonreligious people, leaders as well as followers, so they can fully decode the proofs of the formation of the universe, of life, and of chemicals they have been wanting to demonstrate or grasp.

CHAPTER 4: FORMATION OF ANGELS AND THEIR CONTROL OF CELESTIAL BODIES

The current programs of Science180 Academy are:

1. **SCIENCE180 ACADEMY OF COSMOLOGY** (Designed for all scientists who want to scientifically study cosmology, the science of the origin and fate of the universe)

2. **SCIENCE180 ACADEMY OF TURBULENCE** (This is a perfect fit for scientists and other experts interested in studying abiotic turbulence).

3. **SCIENCE180 ACADEMY OF LIFE SCIENCES** (Tailored to those who want to study biotic turbulence

4. **SCIENCE180 ACADEMY OF CHEMISTRY** (Designed for chemists, biochemists, scientists, and other educated people who want to understand the origin of chemical particles)

5. **SCIENCE180 ACADEMY FOR LAYPEOPLE OR THE GENERAL PUBLIC** (Very fit for any layperson or "less" educated people who wants to learn (in a simple language) deep insights that even those who went to university for years were unable to decrypt by themselves, so these laypeople can be equipped to eliminate all forms of scientific and religious universe-origin prejudices)

6. **SCIENCE180 ACADEMY FOR CHILDREN** (This Academy breaks down origin key topics into language that children can fully understand). This is the only Science180 Academy that your whole family will like and enjoy together, and which will set children on the path of success by accurately showing them early in life the formation of the universe, and how to detect errors in theories or stories that would misguide them as they grow up.

7. **SCIENCE180 ACADEMY OF THE PSEUDEPIGRAPHA AND SPIRITUAL WORLD** (Only one ancient blueprint has the reliable power to help you to accurately decrypt the spiritual origin and history of everything in the universe. If you are a believer and want to delve into the prophetic, angelic, and higher order of knowledge based on the spiritual world, then this Science180 Academy is for you.

8. **SCIENCE180 ACADEMY OF CREATIONISM** (A scientific theory that scientifically explained the origin of the universe, life, and chemicals using turbulence, and that mathematically reconciled science and the Biblical account of creation for the first time in history.

9. SCIENCE180 ACADEMY FOR FREETHINKERS & ALL ANTI-CREATIONISTS (This Science180 Academy is designed for evolutionists, anti-creationists, and all other types of unbelievers seeking to rationally explore and understand alternative arguments for creation or formation or origin of the universe, life, and chemicals from a fresh, scientific perspective).

10. SCIENCE180 ACADEMY OF LEADERSHIP-(Also called "Science180 Academy for Leaders", this program will enlighten leaders of organizations on how to solve their people problems, process problems, and profit problems related to the origin of the universe, of life, and chemicals according to their domain of expertise). With "Science180 Academy of Leadership", leaders will gain new insights so they can cast new visions and avoid focusing on screwed-up processes, products, and services related to universe-origin initiatives that need to be fixed, faced, or dealt with.

Science180 Academy of Leadership will also equip leaders to address process problems related to inefficiency, gaps, missed opportunities, wasted time and efforts, too many steps, bureaucracy, useless layers between organization and customers concerning the innovation, research methodology, research, product development, strategic planning, workforce diversity in alignment with the historic Science180 breakthroughs so that they can sell more often at full price, avoid regrets in the end, open new markets focusing on real solutions …

11. SCIENCE180 ACADEMY FOR GOVERNMENTAL AGENCIES (Do you want to know how and why most nations and governments are wasting millions of dollars on universe-origin and life-origin researches they don't need … and how to avoid it? What if your nation or institution can reduce wasteful spending on universe-origin research and life-origin research, as well as your dependency of wrong theories on the origin of the universe and life?

12. OTHER SCIENCE180 ACADEMY: If you did not relate with any of the Science180 Academies mentioned above, but you are still interested in learning something specific about the origin of the universe, life, and chemicals that better fits your needs, please visit Science180Academy.com to contact us so we can discuss that with you

CHAPTER 5

DISCOVER THE INDESCRIBABLE SECRET LIFE (UNMENTIONED IN THE BIBLE) OF THE FIRST HUMAN BEINGS AND HOW YOU CAN LEARN FROM IT TO IMPROVE YOUR LIFE TODAY

After God created them, Adam and Eve had a great time in the Garden of Eden before sin significantly altered their life. Although the Bible did not disclose the details of the life of Adam and Eve before their fall, the Books of Enoch, the Book of Jubilees, and the Books of Adam and Eve expose these mysteries. As you read this chapter, you will learn how life was in the beginning, and how it could still be if sin had not separated us from God.

5.1. Before his fall, Adam clearly communicated with angels and was in direct contact with heaven

Today, most human beings don't know or believe in angels, and much less how to communicate with them. Many people even deny the existence of heaven. Yet, it was not so in the beginning. Indeed, in the early days of humankind, heaven was continually opened to Adam before his fall.

2 Enoch 31:1 Adam has life on earth, and **I [God]** *created a garden in Eden in the east, so that he should observe the testament and keep the command. 2 I made the heavens open to him, so that he would see the angels singing the song of victory, and the light without shadow. 3 And he was continuously in paradise...*

The First Book of Adam and Eve also showed that before they sinned, Adam and Eve had a bright nature and could see to heaven, even see the angels praising God. Then God told them:

"*When you were under subjection to Me, you had a bright nature within you and for that reason could see distant things* (First Book of Adam and Eve 8:2).

5.2. In the beginning, Adam and Eve did not need water, and the fruits in the Garden of Eden were very big

When Adam and Eve were in the Garden, they did not need or require water, and they did not care about it. The original nature of Adam and Eve did not depend on water like human bodies do today, for God designed it to change if they sinned (First Book of Adam and Eve 10:5-6). As I will explain in the chapter of the sin of Adam and Eve, the first human beings were made of fire. Fire does not need water. Hence, Adam and Eve did not need water before their fall. The aforementioned reference also suggest that Adam and Eve were not supposed to grow like wild animals. It also suggests that angels may not grow like human beings do. As I will detail later in this book, many needs we experience today were not in place in the beginning, but they arose as the initial order established by God was disturbed. In other words, the life originally designed by God was supposed to be very nice. The Garden of Eden was also designed to facilitate life. For instance, fruits in the Garden of Eden, fruits were bigger than fruits outside of it: "*And the weight of each fig was that of a watermelon; for the fruit of the garden was much larger than the fruit of this land*" (First Book of Adam and Eve 41:2).

Furthermore, Adam himself said what life in the Garden was like:

"*9 ... Adam began to pray with his voice before God, and said;— 10 "O Lord, when I was in the garden and saw the water that flowed from under the Tree of Life, my heart did not desire, neither did my body require to drink of it; neither did I know thirst, for I was living .... 11 So that in order to live I did not require any Food of Life, neither did I drink of the Water of Life*" (First Book of Adam and Eve 41: 9-11).

I guess Adam and Eve may have had no clue that they were privileged. Even today, we do not usually appreciate what we have until we lose it. Very often, we neglect to thank God for the rain and the sunshine until we face weeks or months of drought or until the cold whether hit us before we appreciate what we were ingrateful for. When the weather is nice like spring and fall, most people would not appreciate it until it changes to summer or winter.

5.3. In the Garden of Eden, Adam and Eve knew neither night nor day

In the Garden of Eden, Adam and Eve were constantly in light or in the presence of light:

He [Adam] said to her [Eve] "Remember the bright nature in which we lived, when we lived in the Garden! O Eve! Remember that while we were in the Garden, we knew neither night nor day ... Think of that garden in which there was no darkness while we lived in it (First Book of Adam and Eve 11:7-9).

Adam and Eve could have wished that the nice life in the Garden of Eden

CHAPTER 5: LIFE IN THE GARDEN OF EDEN BEFORE ADAM AND EVE SINNED

could have continued, but unfortunately, it was cut short by the fall of angels and humankind. In the next chapter, I will explain how some angels fell in heaven, and then corrupted the Earth, where Adam and Eve were living.

5.4. Wild animals were obedient to Adam and Eve before their fall

Before Adam and Eve sinned, all wild animals were obedient to them. God made wild animals dumb and dull so that men could dominate them. In the Last Days, God will not judge wild animals, but He will hold men accountable for the care they gave them:

2 Enoch 58:1 "Listen to me, my [Enoch's] *children, today. 2 In those days when the Lord came down to earth for Adam's sake, and visited all his creatures, which he created himself, after all these he created Adam, and the Lord called all the beasts of the earth, all the reptiles, and all the birds that soar in the air, and brought them all before the face of our father Adam. 3 And Adam gave names to all things living on earth. 4 And the* **Lord appointed him ruler over all, and subjected all things to him under his hands, and made them dumb and made them dull that they would be commanded by man and be in subjection and obedience to him. 5 The Lord also created every man lord over all his possessions. 6 The Lord will not judge a single soul of beast for man's sake, but He judges the souls of men through their beasts in this world, for men have a special place.**

The First Book of Adam and Eve 7:4 also explained that in the that Adam was obeying God, he named all the animals according to God's mind and they were all subject to Adam.

Another Book by Nathanael-Israel Israel:
TURBULENT ORIGIN OF LIFE

THE ONLY ACCURATE FORMULA TO SCIENTIFICALLY EXPLAIN THE FORMATION OF ALL FORMS OF LIFE QUICKLY

Every human being will benefit from understanding the real origin of life. But the problem is that most efforts to explain the origin of life are complex, inaccurate, confusing, partisan, complicated, therefore, creating serious challenges to those who are eager to scientifically decrypt where all forms of life came from. Most people want an accurate, simple, straightforward, nonpartisan life-origin book that is free from jargons and difficult concepts only known by the experts. This elegant scientific book breaks down the technicality of the origin of life in a language that even the nonscientists can easily comprehend. It is a trustworthy book that will help you to quickly, cheaply, easily, and efficiently navigate everything you need to know to finally decode and solve the puzzling problems about the origin of life, while also giving you a crash course on the universe-origin.

Unlike any book you have ever read on the origin of life, this historic masterpiece (that distills complex scientific data down to simple explanations that make sense) is the starting point of any smart person wanting to rationally understand the formation of all living things. By the time you finish reading *"Turbulent Origin of Life"*, you will discover:

- Why in spite of the massive amount of scientific data collected on living things, scientists have misunderstood the formation of life until now, and then uncover in a simple language the one thing that was needed to accurately crack the code of life but that scientists have missed and that has been causing them headaches, overwhelm, and burnout
- Step-by-step pathway to decode the origin of life and get the power, freedom, and boldness to take advantage of the opportunities that accurate understanding of the origin of life creates (Science180.com/life)
- The high connection between the code of the universe formation and the process by which life on Earth was formed so you can become a fulfilled thought leader in your field of expertise
- Tools to stand as a lighting bolt that electrifies those who are still struggling to understand the formation of all forms of life in the universe
- Strategies to push the boundaries of human abilities to properly understand what is perceived as un-understandable, mysterious, supernatural, unimaginable, impossible, and unthinkable that hold people back

CHAPTER 5: LIFE IN THE GARDEN OF EDEN BEFORE ADAM AND EVE SINNED

- Scientific approach to holistically detect, correct, and remove all misinformation, ambiguity, and misleading claims and theories surrounding the origin of life

Whether you are a scientist or a layperson, a believer, or a skeptic, you cannot afford to ignore the greater, better, faster, simpler, cheaper, easier, and accurate formula unlocked in this important book that successfully decoded the origin of life. Get *"Turbulence Origin of Life"* today and change lives! Don't wait!

Dr. Nathanael-Israel Israel is the Father of Science180 Cosmology and the Founder of Science180 Academy. He is fortunate to be known as the source of unconventional wisdom and knowledge that help people accurately crack the code of the formation of the universe, of life, and of chemicals. Get some resources by visiting his personal website at Israel120.com.

ORIGIN OF THE SPIRITUAL WORLD

CHAPTER 6

DID THE FALL OF THE PRINCE OF THIS WORLD CAUSE THE EARTH TO LOSE ANYTHING AND BECOME A TERRIBLE PLACE WHERE EVIL FORCES DOMINATE?

The circumstances surrounding the sin and fall of Satan is one of the most enigmatic mysteries that even believers have struggled to properly grasp. In this chapter, you will learn how the pseudepigrapha sheds light on that issue. I will present the story as recounted in the Books of Enoch, the Books of Adam and Eve, the Book of Jubilees, and the Biblical Book of Revelations.

6.1. Fall of Satan according to the Books of Enoch

Because Satan, originally an archangel, had the impossible thought of building his throne above the earth and equal to God, he was pushed away. Consequently, he was flying in the air.

2 Enoch 29:4. One of these [angels] *in the ranks of Archangels, having turned away with the rank below him, entertained an impossible idea, that he should make his throne higher than the clouds over the earth, and should be equal in rank to My power. 5. And I* [God] *hurled him from the heights with his angels. And he was flying in the air continually, above the abyss.* (Translation by W.R. Morfill edited by Henry Frowde)

Joseph B. Lumpkin translated the same story as:

2 Enoch 29:3 And one from out the order of angels, having violated the command he was given, conceived an impossible thought, to place his throne higher than the clouds above the earth so that he might become equal in rank to my power. 4 And I threw him out from the height with his angels, and he was flying in the air continuously above the bottomless (abyss). (Translation by Joseph B. Lumpkin)

According to the chronology of the events in the Books of Enoch, the above story (2 Enoch 29) was positioned before the 3rd day, which events are

CHAPTER 6: FALL OF SATAN AND ITS CONSEQUENCES

recorded in 2 Enoch 30, meaning the next chapter. Therefore, based on this chronology, Satan may have fallen no sooner than the second day of creation. Other manuscripts such as the Book of Genesis written by Moses and the book of the prophet Ezekiel give details on the fall of Satan. According to Ezekiel, Satan even did business in the Garden of Eden. But according to 2 Enoch 30:1, the Garden of Eden was planted on Earth on the third day. According to some people, the Garden of Eden was created and placed on the 3rd Heaven, and then planted it on Earth. Although these interpretations seem confusing, they point at the depth of some mysteries which human beings cannot fully comprehend and agree on this Earth until the day all proofs will be given. Yet, I felt like it is important to bring these things up here, for although they may not answer all of our questions, they can help someone to know what could have happened.

Satan did not just fall, but he also orchestrated the fall of Adam and Eve. The second book of Enoch showed that, because Satan was jealous of Adam and Eve, he conspired against them. He seduced Eve, the wife of Adam, who then convinced Adam to eat of the fruit of the "tree of the knowledge of good and evil", which God had instructed Adam not to eat (Genesis 2:16 and Genesis 3:1-8).

2 Enoch 31:3 **And he [Adam] was continuously in paradise, and the devil understood that I wanted to create another world, because Adam was lord on earth, to rule and control it. 4 The devil is the evil spirit of the lower places, he made himself a fugitive from the heavens as the devil and his name was Satan. Thus he became different from the angels, but his nature did not change his intelligence as it applied to his understanding of righteous and sinful things.** *5 And he understood his condemnation and the sin that he had committed before. Therefore, he devised a thought against Adam, in which he entered and seduced Eve, but did not touch Adam. 6 But I [God] cursed ignorance. However, what I had blessed before I did not curse. I did not curse man, nor the earth, nor other creatures. But I cursed man's evil results, and his works.*

In the next chapter, I will explain how Adam and Eve fell, and what happened to them afterwards.

Another Book by Nathanael-Israel Israel:
RECONCILING SCIENCE AND CREATION ACCURATELY

THERE IS ONLY ONE SIMPLE, COMPELLING, SOLUTION-DIRECTED SCIENTIFIC FORMULA ACCURATE ENOUGH TO RATIONALLY EXPLAIN HOW GOD CREATED THE UNIVERSE

"Reconciling Science and Creation Accurately" is a landmark book in universe-origin writing from a rare perspective by one of the most respected minds of our time. It scientifically explores the most challenging questions of all times that believers, nonbelievers, and all freethinkers are interested in: How can we rationally demonstrate, without checking our brain at the door in the name of faith, that God created the universe? How did the universe begin and what processes did God use to create it? Are these processes still operating in the universe or not? Can believers abandon wrong theories if they think it is impossible for science to literally prove the Genesis story, or if they think that science is evil and diametrically opposed to faith, or if they compromisingly embrace scientific theories that contradict the Biblical account of creation written before the scientific era? What can believers do to help the skeptics believe in the Biblical narrative of creation? Lucky you, Dr. Nathanael-Israel Israel successfully navigated all those questions with an accuracy that both scientists and nonscientists have been applauding across the globe. After reading *"Reconciling Science and Creation Accurately"*, you will confidently:

- Scientifically prove the Biblical account of the creation of the universe and the existence of God in a way that makes the head of those who deny God to spin faster than a DJ's turntable
- Know how to rationally talk to anti-creationists, evolutionists, Big Bang proponents, atheists, skeptics, and other freethinkers about the universe-formation and they will beg you to know more about God, the Creator, that they mistakenly rejected

  Discover very accurate, rare, and factual truths about the universe-origin that will save you time and money, and get you much closer to the better and joyful life you want to live today
  Improve your health and faith by knowing that the existence of God can be scientifically justified using Science180 Cosmology and particularly Science180 Creationism
- Enter a new area of freedom and power by crushing the head of and breaking free from the suffocating expectations of all wrong theories that have highjacked secular and religious education, and that have held the Biblical creation captive for almost 3500 years

CHAPTER 6: FALL OF SATAN AND ITS CONSEQUENCES

- Break free from the suffocating expectations of some forms of creationism that have sequestered the mind of some believers for a long time
- Uncompromisingly, intelligently, and scientifically explode the myth of those who, instead of literally taking the Biblical days of creation as 24-hours consecutive days, think that they were millions of years, or were representative of long ages, or that millions of years existed before them or were positioned between them
- Understand the accurate standard to interpret the Biblical account of creation thanks to Science180's breakthrough that transformed science and laid a foundational bedrock for the inerrancy of Scripture

Now that Genesis (the oldest manuscript in the world, written before science and most religions were born) is scientifically proven to be correct (*Science180.com*/biblical), what unstoppable, jaw-dropping paradigm shift will the discovery of the perfect alignment between science and the Bible bring into the religious, rational, and secular world today? Get this thoughtful book now to figure out what happened at the beginning, what is coming up, and why it is time to urgently rethink everything you have been told about the universe-origin so you don't eventually regret! Don't say nobody told you!

Founder of Science180 Academy, **Dr. Nathanael-Israel Israel** is acknowledged worldwide as the discoverer of the all-in-one, proven, and simple scientific formula that accurately cracked the origin of the universe, of life, and of chemicals, and that scientifically unearthed the holy grail at the intersection of science and the Biblical account of creation. Learn more at Israel120.com.

6.2. Fall of Satan according to the First Book of Adam and Eve

The Bible did not detail what happened in heaven for Satan to fall, but the Books of Adam and Eve did:

First Book of Adam and Eve 55:7 *"Then the angels said to Adam, "You obeyed Satan, and ignored the Word of God who created you; and you believed that Satan would fulfill all he had promised you. 8 But now, O Adam, we will make known to you, what came over us though him, before his fall from heaven. 9 He gathered together his hosts, and deceived them, promising to give them a great kingdom, a divine nature; and other promises he made them. 10 His hosts believed that his word was true, so they yielded to him, and renounced the glory of God. 11 He then sent for us—according to the orders in which we*

ORIGIN OF THE SPIRITUAL WORLD

were—to come under his command, and to accept his vain promises. But we would not, and we did not take his advice. 12 Then after he had fought with God, and had dealt frowardly with Him, he gathered together his hosts, and made war with us. And if it had not been for God's strength that was with us, we could not have prevailed against him to hurl him from heaven. 13 But when he fell from among us, there was great joy in heaven, because of his going down from us. For if he had remained in heaven, nothing, not even one angel would have remained in it. 14 But God in His mercy, drove him from among us to this dark earth; for he had become darkness itself and a worker of unrighteousness. 15 And he has continued, O Adam, to make war against you, until he tricked you and made you come out of the garden, to this strange land, where all these trials have come to you. And death, which God brought to him, he has also brought to you, O Adam, because you obeyed him, and trespassed against God." 16 Then all the angels rejoiced and praised God, and asked Him not to destroy Adam this time, for his having sought to enter the garden; but to bear with him until the fulfillment of the promise; and to help him in this world until he was free from Satan's hand".*

The above verses echoed the story in the book of Revelation according to which a war broke out in heaven and under the leadership of Angel Michael, Satan was cast out:

*"And there was war in Heaven: Michael and his angels fought against the dragon; and the dragon fought and his angels, and prevailed not; neither was their place found any more in Heaven. And the great dragon was cast out — that serpent of old called the Devil and Satan, who deceiveth the whole world. He was cast out onto the earth, and his angels were cast out with him. ... Therefore rejoice, ye heavens, and ye that dwell in them! Woe to the inhabitants of the earth and of the sea! For the devil has come down unto you, having great wrath, because he knoweth that he hath but a short time (*Revelation 12:7-9,12)."

The First Book of Adam and Eve (chapter 6:7) also explained why God casted the devil out:

"But the wicked Satan did not keep his faith and had no good intent towards Me, and although I had created him, he considered Me to be useless, and he sought the Godhead for himself. For this, I hurled him down from heaven so that he could not remain in his first estate. It was he who made the tree appear pleasant to your eyes until you ate it by believing his words"."

Likewise, even as of today, people covet evil and useless things until they sin against God before their eyes open to understand that what they were longing for cannot satisfy them or align them with God. Certainly, Adam and Eve did not know that Satan was lying to them, It was after they faced the "irreversible" consequences rendered by God that they could have fully understood. Similarly, some people reject God today, but will understand their mistakes very late in hell, where there could be no way to change their destiny. Some people blame God as evil because they think he punishes sins, but in the beginning of creation, God did not plan to destroy His creatures:

"I am God the creator who, when I created My creatures, did not intend to destroy them. But after they had greatly roused My anger, I punished them with grievous plagues until

CHAPTER 6: FALL OF SATAN AND ITS CONSEQUENCES

they repent. But if on the contrary they still continue hardened in their transgression, they shall be under curse forever" (First Book of Adam and Eve 6:9-10).

In other words, pains inflicted by God should wake people up and cause them to seek Him. Unfortunately, that is not usually the case as most people continue to disobey God by dwelling in their sins, not knowing that they are setting themselves up for eternal punishment.

6.3. Before the fall, the snake used to be the most beautiful animal, but after the fall, it became the least and the meanest of all animals

The snake was changed after God cursed it:

First Book of Adam and Eve *17:2 But as they [Adam and Eve] went near it, before the western gate, from which Satan came when he deceived Adam and Eve, they found the serpent that became Satan coming at the gate, and sorrowfully licking the dust, and wiggling on its breast on the ground, by reason of the curse that fell on it from God. 3 And whereas before the serpent was the most exalted of all beasts, now it was changed and become slippery, and the meanest of them all, and it crept on its breast and went on its belly. 4 And whereas it was the fairest of all beasts, it had been changed, and was become the ugliest of them all. Instead of feeding on the best food, now it turned to eat the dust. Instead of living, as before, in the best places, now it lived in the dust. 5 And, whereas it had been the most beautiful of all beasts, all of which stood dumb at its beauty, it was now abhorred of them. 6 And, again, whereas it lived in one beautiful home, to which all other animals came from elsewhere; and where it drank, they drank also of the same; now, after it had become venomous, by reason of God's curse, all beasts fled from its home, and would not drink of the water it drank; but fled from it* (First Book of Adam and Eve 17:3-5).

6.4. Why God muted snakes

Of all the main animals in the bush, snakes are the only one that does not make a clear sound. They just sound like a "Ssssssssssssssss". I never knew God had muted them after the snakes continued attacking Adam and Eve, even after the fall, until I came across the reason in the First Book of Adam and Eve 18:1-8:

"*1 When the accursed serpent saw Adam and Eve, it swelled its head, stood on its tail, and with eyes blood-red, acted like it would kill them. 2 It made straight for Eve, and ran after her; while Adam standing by, cried because he had no stick in his hand with which to hit the serpent, and did not know how to put it to death. 3 But with a heart burning for Eve, Adam approached the serpent, and held it by the tail; when it turned towards him and said to him:— 4 "O Adam, because of you and of Eve, I am slippery, and go on my belly." Then with its great strength, it threw down Adam and Eve and squeezed them, and tried to kill them. 5 But God sent an angel who threw the serpent away from them, and raised them up. 6* **Then the Word of God came to the serpent, and said to it,**

ORIGIN OF THE SPIRITUAL WORLD

"The first time I made you slick, and made you to go on your belly; but I did not deprive you of speech. 7 This time, however, you will be mute, and you and your race will speak no more; because, the first time My creatures were ruined because of you, and this time you tried to kill them." 8 Then the serpent was struck mute, and was no longer able to speak."

The book of Jubilees went further to clarify that on the day that God punished the snake, Adam, and Eve, He removed speech from all animals for they used to communicate with Adam and Eve before:

Jubilees 3:23 *And on that day on which Adam came out of the garden of Eden he offered, as a sweet savour, a burnt offering: frankincense and galbanum and myrrh spices, in the morning with the rising of the sun, on the day when he covered his shame. 24. And on that day was closed the mouth of all the animals and of the beasts and of the birds and of whatever walks and of whatever moves, so that they could not speak; for they all had spoken with each other one lip and one tongue.' 25. And he sent out of the garden of Eden all flesh that was in the garden of Eden, and all flesh was scattered according to its kinds and according to its natures to the places which had been created for them. 26. And to Adam alone did he give to cover his shame, of all the animals and beasts. 27. On this account it is commanded in the tablets of heaven concerning all who know the judgment of the law, that they shall cover their shame and shall not uncover themselves as the gentiles uncover themselves. 28. And at the new moon of the fourth month Adam and his wife came out of the garden of Eden and dwelt in the land of Elda, in the land of their creation. 29. And Adam called the name of his wife Eve. 30. And they did not have a son until the first jubilee year; and after" this he knew her. 31. But he cultivated the land, as he had been taught in the garden of Eden (Jubilees 3:23-31)."*

Other books in the Bible also suggest that wild animals once spoke clearly:

- Genesis 3:1-4 where the serpent spoke to Eve to deceive her
- Numbers 22:28-30 narrates how God opened up the mouth of Balaam's donkey
- Revelation 5:13 talks about creatures in heaven, on the earth, and under the earth and the sea blessing, honoring, and glorying the Lamb
- Revelation 8:13 where an eagle talked with a loud voice.

Other significant consequences of the fall of Satan are his temptation of Adam and Eve, the corruption of the world by fallen angels, and many other drastic events I will review in the next 2 chapters.

CHAPTER 6: FALL OF SATAN AND ITS CONSEQUENCES

'Science180 Academy' Success Strategy:
SCIENCE180 INTERVIEW REPORT (AKA SCIENCE180 INTERNET-TV-RADIO INTERVIEW REPORT)

Science180 Interview Report is the newsletter to read for guests and unconventional show ideas at the intersection of science and faith. Indeed, many hot questions are still unanswered on the road leading to the correct understanding of the origin of the universe, of life, and of chemicals. But most people don't know where to find the accurate answers to those challenging questions. What if with one simple call you can accurately answer all of those questions. You need to get in touch with or interview Dr. Nathanael-Israel Israel on your show, radio, tv, podcast, and even website, or invite him for a live presentation at your organization if your audience can benefit from any of the following show, talk, speaking, or interview ideas:

- Are most Christians denying the God they want the nonbelievers to accept?
- Can anyone scientifically prove the Bible to be true?
- Can we explain the formation of the universe through natural processes without evoking evolution and Big Bang?
- Can you scientifically demonstrate the Biblical account of creation without mentioning the Bible?
- Does the Bible scientifically teach anything about the universe-origin that most people including Christians ignore?
- How does the Biblical account of creation help to defend the accuracy of the Bible and the existence of God?
- How people, including some fervent Christians, come to believe lies about creation and what they can do to change them so atheists can enjoy God.
- How to find truth, joy, and accuracy at the intersection of the secularly and biblically divided worlds?
- How to scientifically prove that God created the universe without talking about the Bible
- How to scientifically talk about the universe formation and have nonbelievers and all other freethinkers rationally bow to the Biblical inerrancy?
- How to talk to evolutionists, Big Bang proponents, atheists, and all other freethinkers about the universe formation and they will beg you to teach them more about God, the Creator?

ORIGIN OF THE SPIRITUAL WORLD

- Is it a waste of time to attempt to prove the Biblical creation using science or historical investigation?
- Is it possible to scientifically demonstrate without opening or quoting the Bible that God created the universe?
- Is science making you doubt God or the Bible?
- Is science really at war with religion?
- Is your church or pastor making you doubt God or the Biblical creation?
- Is your school teaching about the universe-origin making you doubt creation?
- What are the 4 surprising essential skills for smart people to crack the universe-origin?
- What are the 7 Biblical Genesis details that seem bogus and stupid but really do scientifically defend the Biblical account of creation?
- in evolutionism, Big Bang, and other theories that deny God.
- Why are most nations (governments) wasting millions of dollars on universe-origin and life-origin researches they don't need–or do they?
- Why Christians are abandoning wrong creationist theories that compromise with Darwinism and Big Bang?
- Why freethinkers and rationalists enjoyed rejecting the most rational story told before the birth of science and how it affects their search for the truth
- Why you don't have to embrace evolution or deny God to scientifically prove that God created the universe in 6 literal days

I know you may be tempted to answer these questions by yourselves, but avoid landing yourself on wrong paths that caused some people to lose contact with reality, it is better to get the accurate answer from the know-how expert, Dr. Nathanael-Israel Israel, the author of many books on the origin of the universe, of life, and of chemicals, and the standout expert who accurately decoded the scientific formula that forces science to bow to the Scriptures. If you would like to register to Science180 Interview Report so we can periodically send you show ideas and opportunities related to the origin of the universe, of life, and of chemicals particles, please visit Science180Interviews.com for more details. Go to Israel120.com to invite Nathanael-Israel Israel to your organization asap to hear his insights on those interview questions.

CHAPTER 7: SIN OF ADAM AND EVE AND ITS CONSEQUENCES

CHAPTER 7

WHAT IS LIFE ON EARTH SUPPOSED TO BE AND WHY DO HUMAN BEINGS SUFFER TODAY? DID WE OR THE EARTH LOSE ANYTHING WE CANNOT RECOVER?

Why is life on Earth so hard and filled with so many challenges? Has it been that way since the beginning? Did anything in human nature change and no longer exist in human being today? In this chapter, you will discover mysteries about what life was supposed to be and why human beings function in certain ways today!

7.1. Adam and Eve's original sin

The Bible revealed that life was not difficult in the beginning, but only after Adam and Eve had transgressed God's commandment. Although some details about the fall of Adam and Eve were not mentioned in the Bible, some pseudepigraphic scriptures shed light on them:

"And the Lord said to Adam and Eve. "You transgressed at your own free will, until you have come out of the garden in which I had placed you. Of your own free will have you transgressed through your desire for divinity, greatness, and an exalted state, such as I [God] have; therefore, **I deprived you of the bright nature which you had then, and I made you to come out of the garden to this land, rough and full of trouble ... And there were fruits in the garden better than that one** [the one they sinfully ate]*"* (First Book of Adam and Eve 6:4-6).

Although some people think that the forbidden fruit was the best fruit in the Garden of Eden, the above verse said the opposite, for there were better fruits in the Garden of Eden, implying that Adam and Eve disobeyed not because they lacked fruits. They were not supposed to even sit under the forbidden tree, but they went near it, envied it, touched it, questioned God's commandment, and obeyed Satan's lies, just to realize their painful fate too late. Reading only the Bible, we may think that God forbade Adam and Eve only from not eating the fruit of knowledge. But according to the Book of Adam and Eve, God went further to attempt to shield them, but the first human beings fell:

16 Then, concerning the tree, I commanded you not to eat of it. Yet I knew that Satan, who deceived himself, would also deceive you. 17 So I made known to you by means of the tree, not to come near him. **And I told you not to eat of the fruit thereof, nor to taste of it, nor yet to sit under it, nor to yield to it** (First Book of Adam and Eve 13:16-17).

As you will read in this chapter, the consequences of the fall of Adam and Eve go beyond the curse of Satan, the hard labor imposed on human beings (including the labor pain and the sweat to cultivate the land), and the thorns in the field (Genesis 3), etc.

7.2. God did not give Satan power over Adam, but Adam fell under Satan's rule by accepting Satan's counsel

After Adam and Eve obeyed Satan, he did not give them what he promised. According to the Books of Adam and Eve, Satan could have pledged many things to Adam and Eve including giving them a divine nature. Unlike what some people think, Satan did not receive the rulership of this world from God. But it was Adam who gave it away by choosing to obey Satan's command (First Book of Adam and Eve 57:3-10):

3 "But when Adam heard these words from him [Satan], he said to him, **"Can you make me a garden as God made for me? Or can you clothe me in the same bright nature in which God had clothed me? 4 Where is the divine nature you promised to give me? Where is that slick speech of yours that you had with us at first, when we were in the garden?"** *5 Then Satan said to Adam, "Do you think that when I have promised one something that I would actually deliver it to him or fulfill my word? Of course not. For I myself have never even thought of obtaining what I promised. 6 Therefore I fell, and I made you fall by that for which I myself fell; and with you also, whosoever accepts my counsel, falls thereby. 7 But now, O Adam, because you fell you are under my rule, and I am king over you; because you have obeyed me and have transgressed against your God. Neither will there be any deliverance from my hands until the day promised you by your God." 8 Again he said, "Because we do not know the day agreed on with you by your God, nor the hour in which you shall be delivered, for that reason we will multiply war and murder on you and your descendants after you. 9 This is our will and our good pleasure, that we may not leave one of the sons of men to inherit our orders in heaven. 10 For as to our home, O Adam, it is in burning fire; and we will not stop our evil doing, no, not one day nor one*

CHAPTER 7: SIN OF ADAM AND EVE AND ITS CONSEQUENCES

hour".

God Himself later told Adam that He never gave Satan power over him (Adam):

"And, also, to show you Satan's meanness, and his evil works, for ever since you [Adam and Eve] *came out of the garden, he* [Satan] *has not ceased, no, not one day, from doing you some harm.* **But I** [God] **have not given him** [Satan] **power over you"** (First Book of Adam and Eve 63:10).

7.3. Satan's true intention to degrade Adam and Eve from their initial light, glory, and clothing

Adam and Eve may not have understood the reasons why Satan tempted them, but God later showed them Satan's true intention: deteriorate the status of Adam and Eve and caused them to lose their position with respect to God. Shortly after they sinned, Adam and Eve saw changes in their nature. For instance, before Adam and Eve sinned, fire could not burn them, but afterward, it scorched them. As the following verses explain, the nature of fire never changed, but sins have caused human bodies to respond to fire differently than they used to in the beginning. Hence, fire which did not hurt human beings before the original sin has been threatening them afterwards. At many occasions, Satan tried to burn and kill Adam and Eve with fire:

"Then they [Adam and Eve] *both began crying because of the fire that separated them from the cave, and that came towards them, burning. And they were afraid. 9 Then* **Adam said to Eve, "See this fire of which we have a portion in us: which formerly yielded to us, but no longer does so, now that we have transgressed the limit of creation, and changed our condition, and our nature is altered. But the fire is not changed in its nature, nor altered from its creation. Therefore, it now has power over us; and when we come near it, it scorches our flesh** (First Book of Adam and Eve 44:8-9)."

However, chapters 41-43 of the First Book of Adam and Eve explain how the above mentioned fire was put up by the Devil who attempted to warm, even kill Adam and Eve. In short, Satan wished that Adam and Eve degrade their state, and as God confirmed, they indirectly did it.

6 Why, O Adam, has he [Satan] *not kept his agreement with you, not even one day; but* **has deprived you of the glory that was on you**—*when you yielded to his command?* **7 Do you think, Adam, that he loved you when he made this agreement with you? Or that he loved you and wished to raise you on high? 8 But no, Adam, he did not do all that out of love to you; but he wished to make you come out of light into darkness; and from an exalted state to degradation; from glory to abasement; from joy to sorrow; and from rest to fasting and fainting"** (First Book of Adam and Eve 45:4-8).

The above verses also suggest that every time a believer obeys a command of Satan, the later deprives that believer from a glory. People think that it was God who gave Satan the glory which once was upon Adam and Eve. But the above verses suggest that Satan could have stolen the glory and dominion from Adam.

The loss of the original light that was upon Adam and Eve exposed them to detrimental environmental conditions. For example, before they sinned, Adam and Eve did not need clothes, but after their fall, they needed clothes, and until today, all human beings (including those who lost their minds) need clothes. The Bible said that God clothed Adam and Eve with an animal's skin after these first human beings sinned and discovered their nakedness. Revealing more details on the matter, the Books of Adam and Eve disclosed that, since the beginning of human clothing, clothes have been a sign of weakness and of death that humans put on, prophetically reminding them of the token of death on their bodies (First Book of Adam and Eve 52:1-2):

"... *Adam and Eve ... cried before God on account of their creation, and of their bodies that required an earthly covering. 2 Then Adam said to Eve, "O Eve, this is the skin of beasts with which we shall be covered, but when we put it on, behold, we shall be wearing a token of death on our bodies. Just as the owners of these skins have died and have wasted away, so also shall we die and pass away*".

Here, death is not just the physical death, but also the death of many privileges that Adam and Eve had in the Garden. Moreover, before Adam and Eve fell, cherubs used to tremble before them but afterward, it became the reverse. Although most people ignore angels and couldn't physically experience them today, Adam and Eve were very familiar with them and the cherubim used to even tremble before them. But all that changed once sin came in. Hence, after Adam and Eve sinned, cherubim no longer got very close to them as usual. At one occasion after Adam and Eve were evacuated from the Garden of Eden, a cherub wanted to give them fruits, but because Adam and Eve's nature had changed, the cherub had to throw the fruits to them from afar, else he could have burned Adam and Eve (who by then trembled at their presence) with their fire:

"**Then the cherub took two figs and brought them to Adam and Eve. But he threw them to them from a distance; for they might not come near the cherub by reason of their flesh, that could not come near the fire** [of the sword in his hand]. *5 At first, angels trembled at the presence of Adam and were afraid of him. But now Adam trembled before the angels and was afraid of them* (First Book of Adam and Eve 36:4-5)".

In short, human beings have been demoted. The following sums up some of the key consequences of the original in: Chapter 35:1 *Then God looked again at Adam and his crying and groaning, and the Word of God came to him, and said to him:—2 "O Adam, when you were in My garden, you knew neither eating nor drinking; neither faintness nor suffering; neither leanness of flesh, nor change; neither did sleep intrude upon thine eyes. But since you transgressed, and came into this strange land, all these trials are come over you."* (First Book of Adam and Eve 35:1-2).

CHAPTER 7: SIN OF ADAM AND EVE AND ITS CONSEQUENCES

Another Book by Nathanael-Israel Israel:
FROM SCIENCE TO BIBLE'S CONCLUSIONS

THE # 1 UNIVERSE-ORIGIN MASTERPIECE OF ALL TIME ... AND THE MOST ACCURATE SCIENTIFIC FORMULA THAT STOOD AND WILL STAND THE TEST OF TIME AND OF MATHEMATICS

The real reason scientists have been struggling to accurately understand the universe-formation is because they have spent centuries collecting expensive, complicated, and massive amounts of data, but learned very little, if not nothing, about how to unconventionally step back to properly analyze it to decode the universe. Consequently, people learned to collect all kinds of data everywhere to build models and imaginary concepts that betray their discernment, but they never learned to unlearn wrong theories, nor learned how to stop trashing great raw data hidden in theories they dislike or misunderstand, never knew where to find and how to properly combine the fundamental variables without which it is impossible to ever clear the way so their data can properly work for and precisely lead them to the real origin of the universe. How can people abandon the dangerous theories they think are correct because they don't know any better ones?

Lucky you, that is where Dr. Nathanael-Israel Israel, the founder of Science180 (Science180.com) came in to properly reanalyze and put under control these costly, underrated data to provide the accurate and simple solution people have been looking for throughout the ages, but that they have ignored.

In *"From Science to Bible's Conclusions"*, you will:

- Get a world class explanation of the 4 fundamental variables without which it is unquestionably impossible to ever decode the universe-formation scientifically
- Save time and money, and enjoy a life filled with the wonderful peace that the accurate understanding of the universe-origin can create
- Unlock the accurate scientific formula to rationally test the existence of God in a historic way that uncompromisingly satisfies both believers and skeptics (*Science180.com/*public)
- Get all you need to become a knowledgeable person who will never again need anybody else to explain to you the origin of the universe, for, you will fully understand and articulate it yourself and rationally know whether science is really at war with religion

- Receive deep insights that even those who went to university for years were not able to decrypt by themselves, so you can equip yourself to eliminate all forms of scientific and religious universe-origin prejudices
- Discover whether the scientific data finally confirms that the formation of the Earth was completed on the 3rd day, while that of the Moon and the Sun was on the 4th day of creation like the Bible says, or whether the data proves that it took billions of years to progressively form the universe
- Understand the celebrated scientific formula that rationally puts to rest all debates about the relationship between science, faith, and all theories about the universe-origin so you can properly develop yourself, expand your network, and shape your future

Quickly grab and read this scientifically verifiable, bestselling book to finally get the accurate, jaw-dropping answer that has been rationally shaking both believers, skeptics, and all freethinkers. Don't wait!

Dr. Nathanael-Israel Israel has had the honor to be acknowledged as the #1 universe-origin, life-origin, and chemicals-origin expert. He is the author of *"Turbulent Origin of the Universe"*, *"Reconciling Science and Creation Accurately"*, *"Turbulent Origin of Chemical Particles"*, *"Turbulent Origin of Life"*, *"How Baby Universe Was Born"*, *"Science180 Accurate Scientific Proof of God"*. Visit Israel120.com to learn more about this world's most trusted expert that helps scientists and laypeople to properly decode the origin and formation of the universe, life, and chemicals so people can live more effectively nonstop.

7.4. Adam and Eve's eyes changed after they sinned and they could no longer see angels praising in heaven

Now, I will elaborate on what happened to the vision of the first human beings once sin sank in. Indeed, after Adam and Eve transgressed, the spectrum of their eyes was changed and they could no longer clearly see in the spiritual realm as they used to:

*"And Adam said to Eve, "**Look at your eyes, and at mine, which before beheld angels praising in heaven without ceasing. Now, we do not see as we did: our eyes have become of flesh; they could not see like they saw before**"* (First Book of Adam and Eve 4:8-9).

Many things they could easily see before became hidden to them. Then God told them:

*"**When you were under subjection to Me, you had a bright nature within you and for that reason could see distant things. But after you transgressed, your***

CHAPTER 7: SIN OF ADAM AND EVE AND ITS CONSEQUENCES

bright nature was taken out of you and it was not left in you to see distant things, but only things near you, as is the ability of the flesh, for it is brutish" (First Book of Adam and Eve 8:2).

Shortly after this event, God ceased communicating with Adam and Eve (First Book of Adam and Eve 8:4) and began sending them either His word or holy angels to transmit messages. As the story progressed in the Books of Adam and Eve, Adam and Eve ignored many things. After they fell, they asked too many questions to God, who initially answered them all face to face, but who later decided to stop communicating with Adam and Eve face to face. It was as if Adam and Eve were no longer qualified to directly converse with God face to face as they used to before their sins. Today, people pray to God that they cannot see face to face, and they believe He hears them, but in the beginning, it was not like that: Adam and Eve talked to God directly and could see things happening in heaven. How much have we lost by disobeying God? Even in the midst of our sins today, we still have many privileges granted to us by God, but most people ignore them, and some have to lose them before realizing. We need to be more grateful to God.

Before sinning, Adam and Eve not only used to converse with angels, but they were above angels. But after sinning, they could not even see the angels and at some point, they begged them to pray to God on their behalf:

First Book of Adam and Eve 55:2 *"**Then Adam, when he heard the Word of God, and the fluttering of the angels whom he did not see, but only heard the sound of them with his ears, he and Eve cried, and said to the angels:—3 "O Spirits, who wait on God, look at me, and at my being unable to see you! For when I was in my former bright nature, then I could see you. I sang praises as you do; and my heart was far above you. 4 But now, that I have transgressed, that bright nature is gone from me, and I am come to this miserable state.** And now I have come to this, that I cannot see you, and you do not serve me like you used to do. For I have become animal flesh. 5 Yet now, **O angels of God, ask God for me, to restore me to that wherein I was formerly; to rescue me from this misery, and to remove from me the sentence of death He passed on me for having trespassed against Him."** 6 Then, when the angels heard these words, they all grieved over him; and cursed Satan who had misled Adam, until he came from the garden to misery; from life to death; from peace to trouble; and from gladness to a strange land."*

Unfortunately, the holy angels could not satisfy Adam's need, but they told him the story of Satan's fall since Adam may have not known it.

After Adam and Eve sinned, fire, which was not supposed to hurt human beings, for they were made of fire, became one of their harsh enemies. After Adam and Eve fell, Satan used fire to chastised them. At many occasions, Satan spilled it on them. After Satan managed to spill fire on Adam and Eve one day, it burned them, and, while screaming because of the coal-fire burn, they called God for help. He sent an angel to help them, and then, He told them the following (First Book of Adam and Eve 46:4-7):

"And God said to Adam, "See Satan's love for you, who pretended to give you the Godhead and greatness; and, behold, he burns you with fire, and seeks to destroy you from off the earth. 5 *Then look at Me, O Adam; I created you, and how many times have I delivered you out of his hand? If not, wouldn't he have destroyed you?"* 6 *God said again to Eve, "What is that he promised you in the garden, saying, 'As soon as you eat from the tree, your eyes will be opened, and you shall become like gods, knowing good and evil.'* **But look!** *He has burnt your bodies with fire, and has made you taste the taste of fire, for the taste of the garden; and has made you see the burning of fire, and the evil of it, and the power it has over you.* 7 *Your eyes have seen the good he has taken from you, and in truth he has opened your eyes;* *and you have seen the garden in which you were with Me, and you have also seen the evil that has come over you from Satan. But as to the Godhead he cannot give it to you, neither fulfill his speech to you.* **No, he was bitter against you and your descendants, that will come after you."**

In other words, when they were in paradise in the Garden, Adam and Eve did not know the many blessings and privileges they had. They took them for granted until they sinned and were removed from it. Likewise, many people today ignore their privileges and the grace of God. Some acknowledge the blessings they have only after losing them, and regrets set in. Likewise, countless people are denying God today, not knowing that a time is coming when they will look back and regret their decision of unbelief, but unfortunately it will be too late.

7.5. Appearance and significance of darkness

The disappearance of the light of Adam and Eve also means that a darkness appeared on them. For whenever light leaves a place, darkness appears. After Adam and Eve broke the law, darkness fell on them and separated them from one another so much so that they could no longer constantly see each other as they used to in the Garden of Eden (First Book of Adam and Eve 12:9-10). God later explained to Adam why they experienced darkness after sinning:

First Book of Adam and Eve 13:1 …. *He [God]* *said to him [Adam]: 2 O Adam, so long as the good angel was obedient to Me, a bright light rested on him on his hosts, 3 But when he transgressed My commandment, I disposed him of that bright light and he became dark. 4 And when he was in the heavens, in the realms of light, he knew nothing of darkness. 5 But he transgressed and I made him fall from the heaven onto the earth, and it was this darkness that came over him. 6 And, O Adam, while in the garden and obedient to Me, that bright light rest also on you. 7 But when I heard of your transgression, I took from you that bright light.* Yet, of my mercy, I did not

CHAPTER 7: SIN OF ADAM AND EVE AND ITS CONSEQUENCES

turn you into darkness, but I made your body a body of flesh over which I spread this skin in order that it may bear cold and heat. 8 If I had let My wrath fall heavily on you, I should have destroyed you and had turned you into darkness, it would have been as if I had killed you.

This statement means that when Lucifer sinned, God completely removed the light that was originally on him in heavens. Likewise, when Adam sinned, God removed the glorious light that used to shine on him in the Garden of Eden, but God covered Adam's body with a skin, which God did not do for Satan. Hence, human beings have a flesh, while Satan and demons don't. This also implies that human beings as of today are different from what Adam and Eve looked like before they sinned. They were spiritual beings which were constantly living in light as God does until today. For God is light. The above verses also suggest that darkness is a form of death. And because no light is in Satan and demons, they are already "dead". Reading the above story, I felt like in the beginning, the skin of Adam and Eve must have been different from our skin today. Furthermore, after they left the Garden, their next habitation was a cave, where they had to cope with darkness. Knowing that even today, most caves are very dark, I can imagine how Adam and Eve were shocked as they (who used to be filled with light) discovered the darkness of a cave for the first time. It must have been painful!

Because Adam and Eve had not experienced darkness before they fell, God had to teach them that the darkness of the night would last for 12 hours. God then explained to Adam that He made the day and placed the Sun in it so that Adam and his children would do their work, rest on it from their work, and also so that the beasts can go forth and look for their food at night (First Book of Adam and Eve 13:20). For God knew they would sin one day and come out of the Garden of Eden. God initially planned for Adam and Eve to stay in the original light and give birth to children of light (First Book of Adam and Eve 13:10-14), but that plan was screwed by sin.

Moreover, other passages also explained that Lucifer was stripped of his initial glorious image and given a hideous form even since he fell from heaven; and because Satan could not come near Adam in that form, he used to transform himself into an angel of light (First Book of Adam and Eve 27:12-15). Until today, Satan and demons like to hide themselves in other beings and things as they deceive people, for in their real form, they might not scare anybody.

Furthermore, God displayed a very high intelligence by forming things with a limited fire, yet Himself is an unapproachable fire. Indeed, as explained throughout this book, everything that God created has energy and fire stored in them in various ways. God is very smart to use the "same" fire He is made of to form things in nature but to delimit it beforehand by compressing, spiraling, winding it, or making a pile of it in such a way that the energy of the creatures cannot be released completely without destroying or transforming them, and also that the creatures cannot change their location and still remain the same, or come into God's presence in their current form without being transformed or destroyed. Thus, everyone cannot dwell in the presence of God but only the elect or chosen ones to whom God will grant many privileges. Controversially, as of today, God could not visit the Earth in all His glory, else He would have to destroy the Earth just as a big stone cannot fall on an egg without breaking it. So, for God to come to the Earth to redeem humankind, He had to abide by some earthly rules including being born through a woman. But when He will come back a second time on the last day, He will bring His glory!

7.6. After Adam and Eve sinned, their diet changed

In the beginning, Adam and Eve were not made to eat certain things as we do today. But because their bodies were altered by sin, they had to learn how to eat earthly food. God had to make their bodies suitable for it so that they would not die or suffer from eating earthly food they were not supposed to eat. The Books of Adam and Eve revealed that after being casted out of the Garden, Adam and Eve fasted for many days, after which God had to adjust their nature to eat earthly foods:

First Book of Adam and Eve 64:3 *"So, as God commanded them, they went into the cave about sunset. And Adam and Eve stood up and prayed during the setting sun. 4* ***Then they sat down to eat the figs; but they knew not how to eat them; for they were not accustomed to eat earthly food. They were afraid that if they ate, their stomach would be burdened and their flesh thickened, and their hearts would take to liking earthly food. 5 But while they were thus seated, God, out of pity for them, sent them His angel, so they wouldn't perish of hunger and thirst.*** *6 And the angel said to Adam and Eve, "God says to you that you do not have the strength that would be required to fast until death; eat, therefore, and strengthen your bodies; for* ***you are now animal flesh and cannot subsist without food and drink."*** *7 Then Adam and Eve took the figs and began to eat of them. But God had put into them a mixture as of savory bread and blood".*

Chapter 65:6 *"****Then God looked at them, and then fitted them for eating food at once; as to this day; so that they should not perish.*** *7* ***Then Adam and Eve came back into the cave sorrowful and crying because of the alteration of their bodies. And they both knew from that hour that they were altered beings, that all hope of returning to the garden was now lost; and that they could not enter it. 8 For that now their bodies had strange functions; and all flesh that requires food and drink for its existence, cannot be in the garden.*** *9 Then Adam said to Eve, "Behold, our hope is now lost; and so is our trust to enter the garden. We no longer belong to the inhabitants of the garden; but from now on we are earthy and of the dust, and of the inhabitants of the earth. We shall not return to the garden, until the day in which God has promised to save us, and to bring us*

CHAPTER 7: SIN OF ADAM AND EVE AND ITS CONSEQUENCES

again into the garden, as He promised us." 10 Then they prayed to God that He would have mercy on them; after which, their mind was quieted, their hearts were broken, and their longing was cooled down; and they were like strangers on earth. That night Adam and Eve spent in the cave, where they slept heavily by reason of the food they had eaten" (First Book of Adam and Eve 65:6-10).

After they sinned, Adam and Eve (who in the beginning did not need water), could not live without it. When they were in the Garden, they did not need or require water, and they did not care about it, but soon after they left, they had to. God explained to them:

"While you were under my command and were a bright angel, you did not experience this water, but now, that you have transgressed my commencement, you cannot do without water to watch your body and make it grow, for it is now like that of beast and is in want of water" (First Book of Adam and Eve 10:5-6).

This suggests that the original nature of Adam and Eve did not need water like human bodies do today, for God designed it to change when affected by sins. God thought through everything when He was designing human beings so that the punishment of transgression could bring pain over them.

In the 40th chapter of the First Book of Adam and Eve, a broader explanation is given to the needs of Adam and Eve for foods:

Chapter 40:2 *"But when you came to live in this strange land, your fleshly body could not survive on earth without earthly food, to strengthen it and to restore its powers."*

> **'Science180 Academy' Success Strategy**
> **HOW TO RAISE RATIONAL CHILDREN IN OUR MODERN WORLD**
>
> In our modern secular world, and with the many things that kids are taught at school and over which parents have little control once the kids head to public school, parents have a lot to worry about. But it does not have to be that way. Universe-origin and life-origin scientist Dr. Nathanael-Israel Israel has discovered that, more than ever, parents have a crucial responsibility to rationally prepare their kids to have a strong worldview that properly embraces both science and faith, so their kids are not pulled on one side by the secular education and on the other side by religious belief. But how can parents and their children achieve that common goal?
>
> Listen to this Beninese-American scientist and mathematician Dr. Nathanael-Israel Israel to figure it out. Nathanael-Israel is the author of the acclaimed book *"How Baby Universe was Born"*, an easy to understand scientific book primarily written for children age 7-12 years old to help them properly crack the code of the formation of the universe in a language they completely enjoy, and that prepares them to fight any secular or religious theory that may try to rationally drift them away from the reality of everything!
>
> Sample questions that will get answered include the following and many more:
> - How can parents use the latest breakthrough about the universe-origin to rationally raise their kids?
> - How can parents prepare their children from being victims of the danger of wrong theories and dogmas on the origin of life and the universe?
> - What can parents do to shield their children from the influence of religious and scientific beliefs that try to enslave them in the name of reason or faith?
> - Why is wrong science not the only danger of raising rational children, but wrong belief as well?
> - How can we help children to positively navigate the intersection of science and faith?
>
> Learn more at Science180.com/children

7.7. Duration of Adam and Eve's stay in the Garden of Eden

The Bible did not say for how long Adam and Even lived in the Garden of

CHAPTER 7: SIN OF ADAM AND EVE AND ITS CONSEQUENCES

Eden before being evacuated, but the pseudepigraphic scriptures did. The Books of Enoch, the Book of Jubilees, and the Books of Adam and Eve all talked about the fall of Adam and Eve, but they gave seemingly different accounts of the timing of the first sin. Considering the dating in the pseudepigraphic scriptures, Adam and Eve could have stayed in the Garden of Eden for about 5.5 hours to 7 years.

Indeed, according to the Slavonic Book of Enoch, Adam spent about 5.5 hours in the Garden of Eden before he and Eve sinned. Still today, Jews strongly believe that Adam and Even did not spend a full day in the Garden of Eden before being ejected by God after their first disobedience usually labelled as the original sin:

2 Enoch 32:1 I [God] *said to him* [Adam]: *You are earth (dirt), and into the earth from where I took you, you shall go, and I will not destroy you, but send you back from where I took you. 2 Then, I can again receive you at My second presence. 3 And I blessed all my creatures, both physical and spiritual. And Adam* **was five and half hours in paradise. 4 And I blessed the seventh day, which is the Sabbath, on which he rested from all his works.**

Furthermore, according to the First Book of Adam and Eve, Adam and Eve sinned on the 3rd hour after their creation and were removed from the Garden 3 hours later, meaning that they stayed in the Garden for about 6 hours (First Book of Adam and Eve 37:4-5), which I think alludes to the 6 working days in a week, and the 6000 years of the world history before rapture:

First Book of Adam and Eve 37:4 "**But Adam began to pray to God and to beseech Him to give him of the fruit of the Tree of Life, saying thus: "O God, when we transgressed Your commandment at the sixth hour of Friday, we were stripped of the bright nature we had, and did not continue in the garden after our transgression, more than three hours.** *5 But in the evening, You made us come out of it. O God, we transgressed against You one hour, and all these trials and sorrows have come over us until this day. 6 And those days together with this the forty-third day, do not redeem that one hour in which we transgressed!*" (First Book of Adam and Eve 37:4-5).

Adam and Eve would not have even stayed in the Garden of Eden for a full day before falling: "**But you [Adam and Eve] did not keep my commandment for one day until I [God] had finished the creation and blessed everything in it**" (First Book of Adam and Eve 13:15). This verse also corroborates with the Jewish culture which believes that Adam and Eve stayed in the Garden of Eden for just a few hours and fell the same day they were created. This statement seems to agree with what happened to Satan and his angels for, like I explained in other books, they could have sinned the same day they were formed. And the great 5 and half days that God mentioned in First Book of Adam and Eve 7:1-3, and which I will revisit in another chapter very soon, suggested that something could have happened around the middle of the 6th day, which is around day 5 and a half. Adam and Eve may have really fallen on the same day they were created. Because Enoch is the author of the Books of Enoch and also the Books of Adam and Eve, it should not be surprising that their dating of the duration of the stay of Adam and Eve in the Garden of Eden is similar: 5.5 hour to 6 hours.

Moreover, the Book of Jubilees (also called the Little Genesis, or the Apocalypse of Moses, or the Book of the Law and the Testimony), gave a precise date of the temptation of Adam and Eve. Indeed, the Book of Jubilees revealed that Adam was created not in the Garden of Eden, but outside the Garden, in the land of Elda and that God had to wait for 40 days before the angels conducted him into the Garden on the 17th day of the second month. The story continued saying that, while outside the Garden, from Sunday to Friday morning of the second week, the angels brought the beasts, birds, and fish to Adam to be named. Adam then recognized he was different from the beasts. God made him sleep and from Adam's rib, God created the woman, Eve, who had to wait 80 days before being conducted into the Garden of Eden. In the end, the Book of Jubilees mentioned that Adam sinned after being in the Garden of Eden seven years (Book of Jubilees 3:14-17): *"And having ended the completion of seven years which he completed there, in the seventh year exactly, and in the second month, on the seventeenth of the month, the serpent came and approached the woman, and the serpent said to the woman: "Has God commanded that you shall not eat of any of the fruit of the tree in the garden?"* (Translated from the Ethiopic by Rev George H. Schodde).

This account in the Book of Jubilees suggests that the stay of Adam and Eve in the Garden of Eden may have been more than the 5.5-6 hours mentioned in the second Book of Enoch and the Books of Adam and Eve, or that some issues surround these dates or their translation from the original manuscript. As I studied the pseudepigrapha, I noticed that, in general, some dates may be incorrect. Yet, I did not let the dating mismatches to distract me from withdrawing key information from these old and still actual texts.

7.8. After the fall, wild animals turned against Adam and Eve

The fall of humankind also affected wild animals, which were supposed to live under the domination of human beings. After Adam and Eve sinned, Adam quickly sensed that all animals will turn against them and devour them. Therefore, Adam petitioned to God to preserve their life. In His pity for Adam and Eve, God commanded all animals to move to Adam and be familiar with him. All animals did so and paid homage to Adam except for the serpent (against which God was angry) which did not come to Adam with the beasts (First Book of Adam and Eve 7:5-9).

On top of the rebellion and attack of the Devil, creatures, which originally

CHAPTER 7: SIN OF ADAM AND EVE AND ITS CONSEQUENCES

obeyed Adam, have turned against him after the original sin. By doing so, creatures may not be necessarily sinning, but just fulfilling God's commandment and decree. As God told Adam and Eve, after the fall, every creature rose against them:

"*When you were under My control, all creatures yielded to you; but after you have transgressed My commandment, they all rise over you. 5 God said again to him, "See, O Adam, how Satan has exalted over you! He has deprived you of the Godhead, and of an exalted state like Me*, and has not kept his word to you; but has, after all, become your enemy" (First Book of Adam and Eve 45:4-5).

Although many animals have been rebelling against and revolting over human beings after the fall of Adam and Eve (who lost their dominion over wild animals), I think that many animals (i.e. clean animals) are still obeying God. I discussed those mysteries in another book.

7.9. God will not judge wild animals, but they will give account to God about how men treated them

While God will judge human beings in the last days, wild animals will not be" (*2 Enoch 58:7*):

And as every soul of man is according to number, similarly beasts will not perish, nor all souls of beasts which the Lord created, until the great judgment, and they will accuse man, if he did not feed them well.

Wild animals also deserve some rights and it is by ignorance that some people mistreat them. Therefore, as God said, it is better for men not to mistreat wild animals.

2 Enoch 59: **1 Whoever defiles the soul of beasts, defiles his own soul. 2 For man brings clean animals to make sacrifice for sin, that he may have cure for his soul.** *3 And if they bring clean animals and birds for sacrifice, man has a cure. He cures his soul. 4 All is given you for food, bind it by the four feet, to make good the cure.* **5 But whoever kills beast without wounds, kills his own souls and defiles his own flesh. 6 And he who does any beast any injury whatsoever, in secret, it is an evil practice, and he defiles his own soul.**

If wild animals are so priceless before God, how much more are human beings who God created in His own image? I also might add that, throughout history, some people groups have mistreated other people, tribes, and nations. I treated those racial issues in another book of mine. We need to care for all God's creatures, and as we do, we also need to care for God Himself first. For it is unfortunate that some people care for animals, plants, and other forms of life that God created, but they refuse to believe in God. What a mistake!

Another Book by Nathanael-Israel Israel:
TURBULENT ORIGIN OF THE UNIVERSE

THE FIRST AND ONLY SCIENTIFIC BOOK THAT ACCURATELY EXPLAINS EVERYTHING YOU NEED TO UNCONVENTIONALLY, EASILY, AFFORDABLY, AND ENJOYABLY DECODE THE UNIVERSE FORMATION

In *"Turbulent Origin of the Universe"*, filled with great diagrams and digestible scientific facts, you will discover, learn, or get:

- The all-in-one, proven & uncomplicated scientific formula that accurately decoded the formation of the universe, and that explained the birthdate of the stars, planets, satellites, asteroids, and all other celestial bodies in the universe, so you can position yourself to stay on top of your competitors, avoid repeating crucial mistakes that many people have ignorantly made at their own perils

  Extraordinary, unprecedented, accurate insights into the first factors (e.g. early universe physics) that defined the history and formation of the universe so you can tap into deep scientific secrets you ignore, and set yourself apart from others

  The new physics that will revolutionize science forever and land you into a zone of original ideas that improve lives nonstop regardless of your expertise

- The 4 simple things without which it is impossible for anyone to ever understand the formation of the universe, think accurately, work differently, achieve, or perform better for superior results

- The verified key to move the cosmological mountains of misunderstanding, so you can confidently free your mind from doubts, improve your health, and prevent you from any danger connected with sticking with wrong assumptions

- Save time and money, and enjoy your life once you remove errors holding your true understanding of the universe-origin captive

- Historic scientific proof of whether a planet was formed in 2.82 days, whether a satellite was formed in 3.32 days, and whether a star was formed in 3.69 days after the beginning of the universe; so you can creatively produce and address a broader work spectrum by learning how to effectively communicate with and establish unusual connections between otherwise disconnected and disparate scientific data

CHAPTER 7: SIN OF ADAM AND EVE AND ITS CONSEQUENCES

- The scientific formula that successfully tested the existence of God in a way that shocked believers, skeptics, and all other freethinkers
- Why the scientific community has failed to sufficiently explain the origin of the universe; and understand how existing theories have missed and undefined central ideas, and imposed limits on the vision of scientists
- Specific in-depth knowledge, up-to-the-minute information, and ideas so you can expand your market, cut useless costs, stop wasting time on inadequate projects, and start focusing on the profitable solutions (Science180.com/scientific)
- How Science180 Academy can strategically enlighten you, guide you to navigate and filter the massive data collected on the universe, so you can answer the world's most challenging questions, remove any scientific and philosophical cataracts that may be blocking you, and bring you many steps closer to your best life
- How to better resonate with your target market that is craving something original that breaks wrong explanations of the universe-origin

Get *"Turbulent Origin of the Universe"* today to begin an incredible journey of accurately decoding the universe and change your life forever!

Dr. Nathanael-Israel Israel is told by people that he is the #1 Universe-origin, Life-origin, and Chemicals-origin Expert. He is the founder of Science180 and the author of many books on the origin of the universe and its content. To learn more about how he may help you, visit Israel120.com.

CHAPTER 8

WHY AND HOW DID SOME ANGELS DELIGHT IN CORRUPTING THE EARTH KNOWING THAT THEY WOULD EVENTUALLY PAY A HUGE PRICE–OR DIDN'T THEY FOREKNOW WHAT IS AWAITING THEM?

When Satan fell, many angels followed him to disobey God. In general, these angels are called fallen angels or demons, and Satan (also called the Devil) is their chief. Here, I will revisit some of the things they taught human beings as they corrupted the world long after Adam and Eve.

8.1. Corruption of the earth by fallen angels and their judgment

Unlike holy angels who still serve God and minister to human beings, fallen angels did not obey God. The fallen angels bound themselves with an oath before they disobeyed God. Among other things, they slept with women, an immoral event that was also recorded in the Bible (Genesis 6) occurred many years after the formation of the universe and life, and Enoch detailed it more than anyone else:

1 Enoch 6:*2 And the Angels, the sons of Heaven, saw them [women] and desired them. And they said to one another: "Come, let us choose for ourselves wives, from the children of men, and let us beget, for ourselves, children." 3 And Semyaza, who was their leader, said to them: "I fear that you may not wish this deed to be done and that I alone will pay for this great sin." 4 And they all answered him, and said: "Let us all swear an oath, and bind one another with curses, so not to alter this plan, but to carry out this plan effectively." 5 Then they all swore together and all bound one another with curses to it. 6 And they were, in all, two hundred and they came down on Ardis, which is the summit of Mount Hermon. And they called the mountain Hermon because on it they swore and bound one another with curses. 7 And these are the names of their leaders: Semyaza, who was their*

CHAPTER 8: CORRUPTION OF THE EARTH BY FALLEN ANGELS

leader, Urakiba (Araqiel), Rameel, Kokabiel, Tamiel, Ramiel, Daniel, Ezeqiel, Baraqiel, Asael, Armaros, Batariel, Ananel, Zaqiel, Samsiel, Satariel, Turiel, Yomiel, Sariel. 8 These are the leaders of the two hundred Angels and of all the others with them.

In 1 Enoch 69:2, the spelling of the name of some fallen angels changed and new names were added: *Semyaza (Azza), Artaqifa, Armen, Kokabiel, Turiel, Ramiel, Daniel, Nuqael, Baraqiel, Azazel, Armaros, Batriel, Basasael, Ananel, Samsiel, Yetarel, Tumiel, Rumiel, Azazel*". According to second Book of Enoch, Enoch saw the watchers (also called fallen angels) in the 2nd and 5th heaven, while he was on his way to the throne of God. Probably, the story of watchers described in 1 Enoch happened during Enoch's transit in the second heaven.

According to the Books of Enoch, once they corrupted the earth, fallen angels taught human beings charms, spells, fighting, war, root cutting, acquaintance with plants, etc. The giants *"began to sin against birds, animals, reptiles, and fish, and they devoured one another's flesh, and drank the blood from it"* (1 Enoch 7:5), meaning that evil spirits in the fallen angels corrupted also other living organisms on earth. The fallen angels *"taught men to make swords, knives, shields, breastplates. They showed them metals of the earth and the art of working them, the art of making up eyes and of beautifying the eyelids, and the most precious stones, all kinds of coloring and dyes, casting of spells and counter-spells, astrology, constellations, knowledge of the clouds, the signs of the earth, the signs of the sun, the course of the moon, etc."* (1 Enoch 8:1-3). Rebelling against God, these fallen angels taught men how to write with ink and paper, *"for men were not created that they should confirm their faith with pen and ink* (1 Enoch 69:9-11". To make a long story short, fallen angels have taught men evil things that may not have ever crossed human minds or imagination, revealed to men eternal secrets that were made for Heaven only, and they have filled the earth with blood and iniquities (1 Enoch 9:6). In other words, there are things human beings do today that were so advanced than what modern science could have discovered, but which were passed onto humankind by angels who learned those things in their original state before their fall. This corruption of the earth angered God just as Moses mentioned in Genesis 6.

One of the leaders of the fallen angels is called Azazel. He was subsequently punished by God who ordered Archangel Raphael to bury him in a desert until the judgment day (1 Enoch 10:4-6), suggesting that some deserts on earth may be hosting imprisoned fallen angels. According to 1 Enoch 14:4-5, fallen angels are already judged and since their fall, they have no more access to heaven. Fallen angels were originally created clean and spiritual and were dwelling in heaven. As emphasized by Jesus (Luke 20:34), angels were not supposed to marry and procreate like human beings. They were supposed to serve men under the authority of God. However, fallen angels turned against God and have been harming human beings that they failed to serve. Although fallen angels lived in heaven at one point, all the mysteries of heaven were not revealed to them (1 Enoch 16:3). Even the Bible revealed that God has hidden a lot of secrets from the angels who serve Him. Although angels are powerful, and can even transform themselves into man (1 Enoch 17:1-2) and other beings and things, they ignore many heavenly secrets.

God has already judged evil spirits. When a person dies, his or her spirit goes to a special place. The spirit of a dead person can speak and petition to God (1 Enoch 22:3-6). The place where the spirits of the believers in God go to after their death is different from that of the spirits of the unbelievers. Spirits of unbelievers wait in pain for their judgment. On Judgment Day, spirits of men will not be destroyed (1 Enoch 22:9-13), even the spirits of those who will inherit hell. In 2 Enoch 7 and 10, a deep explanation is given about hell and those who will inherit it. In contrast, 2 Enoch 8-9 talks about paradise and those who will go there. The book of Revelation in the Bible also tremendously talks about the Judgement Day.

Enoch also revealed that, just as human beings and angels, nonliving matters can sin. For instance, Enoch disclosed that some stars have transgressed God's commandment and consequently, they are imprisoned (1 Enoch 21:1-7). In the case of nonliving things, which some human beings can perceive as "lacking" a free will, a transgression may not mean a voluntary act of disobedience as we know it, but maybe an inability to become something because of certain constraints. However, I think that wild animals and even nonliving things have their own "language" through which they communicate among themselves in ways that human beings cannot understand, hence human beings think that they are the only ones that can communicate.

8.2. Nephilim (offspring of the mating between fallen angels and women) filled the earth with violence and abominations

I first learned about the existence of the Books of Enoch during a speech given by L.A. Marzulli at the Church of His Presence (in Mobile, Alabama, USA) which was founded and, at the time of the publication of this book, is still led by Pastor John Kilpatrick. During his speech, Mr. Marzulli talked about UFOs and giants such as the Nephilim. Beside the Books of Enoch, the Book of Genesis written by Moses also described how the fallen angels and the giant offspring they begot after sleeping with women corrupted the world. Called Nephilim, these giants are well described in the Bible and in the Books of Enoch. Even in the New Testament, Apostle Jude (the brother of Jesus) mentioned them in his writing. The Nephilim were offspring of the "sons of God or fallen angels" and the "daughters of men" before the flood. They were not angels, nor mere human beings or ordinary children, but a kind of hybrid or violent superhuman offspring but born from the unnatural union between angels and human beings. Although the fallen angels were

CHAPTER 8: CORRUPTION OF THE EARTH BY FALLEN ANGELS

created perfect by God and were perfect before their fall, they rebelled against God as they "forsook their proper dwelling place" in heaven, materialized themselves into human bodies, and "began taking as wives all whom they chose"? (Jude 6; Genesis 6). Mighty ones of old times, very wicked and evil, they filled the earth with violence, and were one of the reasons God flooded the earth during the time of Noah (Genesis 6:1-8):

Genesis 6:1 *"Now when humankind began to multiply on the face of the ground and daughters were born to them, 2 then the sons of God saw that the daughters of men were good and they took for themselves wives, any they chose. 3 Then Adonai said, "My Spirit will not remain with humankind forever, since they are flesh. So, their days will be 120 years. 4* **The Nephilim were on the earth in those days, and also afterward, whenever the sons of God came to the daughters of men and gave birth to them. Those were the mighty men of old, men of renown.** *5 Then Adonai saw that the wickedness of humankind was great on the earth, and that every inclination of the thoughts of their heart was only evil all the time. 6 So Adonai regretted that He made humankind on the earth, and His heart was deeply pained. 7 So Adonai said, "I will wipe out humankind, whom I have created, from the face of the ground, from humankind to livestock, crawling things and the flying creatures of the sky, because I regret that I made them." 8 But Noah found favor in Adonai's eyes"* (Tree of Life Version).

God did not destroy all of the fallen angels during the Great Flood. The book of Jubilees for instance mentioned that God allowed some fallen angels to remain after the flood in the forms of demons, even until the Judgement Day. If God had not reduced their number, fallen angels could have already put the world in the same mess they did before the flood. Some of the Nephilim who remained on earth after the flood have given a lot of problems to the Israelites, including when they tried to conquer the Promised Land, and even afterwards. In the Book of Numbers, Moses recounted that the Nephilim took control of Canaan, known today as Israel, and they had to be overthrown during the conquest of the Promised Land by the Children of Israel (known as Bnei-Yisrael in the Hebrew language and as Jews or Israelites in present day terms):

Bible's Book of Numbers 13:1 *"Adonai spoke to Moses saying, 2* **Send some men on your behalf to investigate the land of Canaan, which I am giving to Bnei-Yisrael** *... 3 So according to the word of Adonai, Moses sent them from the wilderness of Paran ... 17 As he sent them to explore the land of Canaan, he said to them, "Go up there through the Negev, then go up into the hill country. 18 See what the land is like and the people living there, whether they might be strong or weak, few or many. 19 In what kind of land are they living? Is it good or bad? Also, what about the cities in which they are living? Are they unwalled or do they have fortifications? 20 How is the soil—fertile or poor? Are there trees on it or not? Do your best to bring back some of the fruit of the land." 21 So they went up and explored the land from the wilderness of Zin as far as Rehob the entrance of Hamath. 22 They continued on up through the Negev and came to Hebron. There lived Ahiman, Sheshai, and Talmai,* **descendants of Anak.** *23*

ORIGIN OF THE SPIRITUAL WORLD

When they reached as far as the Valley of Eshcol, they cut a single branch with a cluster of grapes. It was carried on a pole between two of them. They also cut some pomegranates and some figs. 24 That place was called the Valley of Eshcol because of the cluster cut by Bnei-Yisrael. 25 They returned from investigating the land after 40 days. 26 **They traveled and returned to Moses, Aaron and the entire community of Bnei-Yisrael at Kadesh in the wilderness of Paran. They gave their report to them and the entire assembly. They showed the land's fruit. 27 They gave their account to him and said, "We went into the land where you sent us. Indeed, it is flowing with milk and honey—this is some of its fruit. 28 Except, the people living in the land are powerful, and the cities are fortified and very large. We even saw the sons of Anak there!** *29 Amalek is living in the land of the Negev, the Hittites, Jebusites, and Amorites are living in the mountains, and the Canaanites are living near the sea and along the bank of the Jordan." 30* **Then Caleb quieted the people before Moses, and said, "We should definitely go up and capture the land, for we can certainly do it!" 31 But the men who had gone up with him said, "We cannot attack these people, because they are stronger than we." 32 They spread among Bnei-Yisrael a bad report about the land they had explored, saying, "The land through which we passed to explore devours its residents. All the people we saw there are men of great size! 33 We also saw there the Nephilim. (The sons of Anak are from the Nephilim.) We seemed like grasshoppers in our eyes as well as theirs!"** (Tree of Life Version).

Today, many demons act through technologies and other means that blind people from knowing the truth. I handled those issues in other books.

CHAPTER 8: CORRUPTION OF THE EARTH BY FALLEN ANGELS

Another Book by Nathanael-Israel Israel:
SCIENCE180 ACCURATE SCIENTIFIC PROOF OF GOD

THE FIRST AND THE ONLY SCIENTIFIC BOOK THAT TALKS TO ANTI-CREATIONISTS, EVOLUTIONISTS, BIG BANG PROPONENTS, ATHEISTS, AND ALL OTHER FREETHINKERS AND RATIONALISTS ABOUT THE UNIVERSE FORMATION AND THEY BEG TO KNOW MORE ABOUT GOD, THE CREATOR, THAT THEY DENY.

As you read this historic book, you will:

- Scientifically know what is the one clear sign you should always pay attention to in your efforts to decipher the primary cause and the key drivers of the fundamental processes responsible for the universe-formation
- Discover the only way to scientifically know if God exist, and if so, which of the thousands of beings worshipped across the globe is the true God
- Accurately answer the most critical universe-origin and life-origin questions so you can stop standing in tension with consequential question marks including those related to religion and reason or the so-called war between science and the Bible
- Discover the errors in the scientific and religious theories about the universe-origin and life-origin that are putting you at a high risk you will never recover from if you don't quickly and confidently learn how to rationally take control over threats lurking at the edge of your efforts to understand the universe and life today
- Definitively answer all your doubts about the source or author of the universe and life … (learn more at Science180.com/godproof)
- Understand that religion or faith, reason or science can coexist and can be properly reconciled to accurately lead you to the correct source of everything in the universe
- Satisfy your burning desire for freedom from beliefs and scientific theories about the universe-origin and life-origin that suffocate you and bind your mind, faith, unbelief, heart, and education
- Scientifically set on fire all false theories or dogmas about the existence of God, the Creator, that are enslaving humankind

- Challenge the cosmological status quo and embrace the real change that will disrupt the hidden cages that may be holding you and that you ignore

Whether you are a believer, unbeliever, freethinker, administrator, politician, curriculum designer, curriculum specialist, education policymaker, teacher, librarian, school board member, researcher, parent, student, clergy, or a layperson, as long as you are really seeking to scientifically understand the rational proof of the existence of God, *"Science180 Accurate Scientific Proof of God"* is the much-admired book written for great people just like you! Grab your copy today and start reading it! Don't wait any longer!

Dr. Nathanael-Israel Israel is a Beninese-American scientist, entrepreneur, and international consultant, who shows people of all ages and educational backgrounds how to scientifically decode the formation of the universe and of life, and who is acknowledged as the creator of the Chemicals Turbulent Origin Formula™, the inventor of the Life Turbulent Origin Formula™, and the discoverer of the Universe Creation Formula™. He is the Founder of Science180 Academy, which is trailblazing the reconciliation between science and the creation.

CHAPTER 9

HOW THE FIRST HUMAN BEINGS WERE BAILED OUT OF THEIR GIGANTIC MISTAKE THAT WOULD HAVE TOTALLY DISCONNECTED THEM FROM THE UTTERMOST JOY FOREVER (AND HOW YOU TOO CAN AVOID CRASHING YOUR LIFE)

God did not just punish Adam and Eve after their sin or leave them in a perdition state forever, but He also shared with them the plan of salvation for themselves and their children. In this chapter, I will reveal how God has been dealing with the plan of redemption since the beginning.

9.1. The promise of salvation to Adam and his descendants

The agenda of Satan did not stop after he defeated the first human beings. The root of the continual schemes and attack of the Devil on humankind is related to the salvation God promised to Adam and his progeny. Indeed, after Adam and Eve were casted out of the Garden of Eden, Satan continued to tempt them, trying to kill them. In other words, one of the reasons Satan attacked Adam and Eve and continues to attack most human beings today is that he sought and still seeks to destroy them and overtake the earth so he can rule it with demons:

First Book of Adam and Eve 47:7 *"But Satan, the hater of all good, thought within himself: "Whereas God has promised salvation to Adam by covenant, and that He would deliver him out of all the hardships that have befallen him—but has not promised me by covenant, and will not deliver me out of my hardships; no, since He has promised him that He should make him and his descendants live in the kingdom in which I once was—I will kill Adam. 8 The earth shall be rid of him; and shall be left to me alone; so that when he*

ORIGIN OF THE SPIRITUAL WORLD

is dead, he may not have any descendants left to inherit the kingdom that shall remain my own realm; God will then be wanting me, and He will restore it to me and my hosts."

These verses showed the stupidity of Satan who thinks that God will want him and restore the Earth to him and his hosts if he (Satan) could manage to kill Adam and Eve and their descendants. But God needs nothing from Satan, not even from his creatures except that they should obey Him and follow His commandments so He can redeem them. But most of them chose to disobey God.

One day, Satan persisted in his rebellion and plan to kill Adam and Eve by throwing a rock onto them when they were sleeping. But because of God's grace, the big stone that Satan threw onto Adam and Eve became a tent (First Book of Adam and Eve 48). When they woke up from their sleep, Adam and Eve did not know what happened to them and, as they found themselves under a tent, they thought that God had punished them by sealing them into a prison to kill them. As they prayed to seek an explanation from God, He told them the following, alluding to the death and resurrection of Jesus Christ:

First Book of Adam and Eve 49:1 *"Then the Word of God came and said:— 2 "O Adam, who counseled you, when you came out of the cave, to come to this place?" 3 And Adam said to God, "O Lord, we came to this place because of the heat of the fire that came over us inside the cave." 4 Then the Lord God said to Adam, "O Adam, you dread the heat of fire for one night, but how will it be when you live in hell? 5 Yet, O Adam, don't be afraid, and don't believe that I have placed this dome of rock over you to plague you with it. 6 It came from Satan, who had promised you the Godhead and majesty. It is he who threw down this rock to kill you under it, and Eve with you, and thus to prevent you from living on the earth. 7 But, in mercy for you, just as that rock was falling down on you, I commanded it to form a dome over you; and the rock under you to lower itself. 8 And this sign, O Adam, will happen to Me at My coming on earth: Satan will raise the people of the Jews to put Me to death; and they will lay Me in a rock, and seal a large stone over Me, and I shall remain within that rock three days and three nights. 9 But on the third day I shall rise again, and it shall be salvation to you, O Adam, and to your descendants, to believe in Me. But, O Adam, I will not bring you from under this rock until three days and three nights have passed." 10 And God withdrew His Word from Adam. 11 So Adam and Eve lived under the rock three days and three nights, as God had told them. 12 And God did so to them because they had left their cave and had come to this same place without God's order. 13 But, after three days and three nights, God created an opening in the dome of rock and allowed them to get out from under it. Their flesh was dried up, and their eyes and hearts were troubled from crying and sorrow".*

9.2. The Lord's prayer we pray today is a prayer first made by Adam and Eve after their fall

The 23rd chapter of the First Book of Adam and Eve indicates that Adam and Eve used to sing praises to God in the Garden of Eden. The first prayer

CHAPTER 9: COVENANT TO REDEEM ADAM, EVE, AND THEIR OFFSPRING

mentioned in their book alludes to the Lord's prayer:

Chapter 23:9 *And Adam began to make more requests of God. Our Father, Who art in Heaven, be gracious unto us, O Lord our God, hallowed be Your Name, and let the remembrance of Thee be glorified in Heaven above and upon earth here below. Let Your kingdom reign over us now and forever. The Holy Men of old said remit and forgive unto all men whatsoever they have done unto me. And lead us not into temptation but deliver us from the evil thing; for Thine is the kingdom and Thou shalt reign in glory forever and forevermore, AMEN* (First Book of Adam and Eve 23:9).

Because this book was written and known before the common era, the similarity between this prayer and the one Jesus taught his disciples suggests that the Lord Jesus was aware of the Book of Adam and Eve, and He was the one who inspired Adam and Eve to say this prayer after their fall.

Moreover, after leaving the Garden of Eden, Adam and Eve fasted for 42 days, and then appealed to God for food and drink while recounting the story of their stay in the Garden (First Book of Adam and Eve 34:1-24). The 42 days of fasting of Adam and Eve could have been the source of the 40 days of fasting and prayer that some people do today

9.3. How and why God promised Adam and Eve that He will visit Earth one day and shed His own blood for the remission of sins, prophetically alluding to the life and death of Jesus Christ

Chapter 21 of the First Book of Adam and Eve explains how Adam and Eve, in their pain and regret of their sin, ended up wounding themselves and shedding their blood. In chapter 23, they built an altar and offered their blood to God for the remission of their sins. First Book of Adam and Eve 24:1-7 elaborated on God's response to their request with a promise of forgiveness of their sins and salvation:

Chapter 24:1 *Then the merciful God, good and lover of men, looked at Adam and Eve, and at their blood, which they had held up as an offering to Him; without an order from Him for so doing. But He wondered at them; and accepted their offerings. 2 And God sent from His presence a bright fire that consumed their offering. 3 He smelled the sweet savor of their offering and showed them mercy. 4 Then came the Word of God to Adam, and said to him, "O Adam, as you have shed your blood, so will I shed My own blood when I become flesh of your descendants; and as you died, O Adam, so also will I die. And as you built an altar, so also will I make for you an altar of the earth; and as you offered your blood on it, so also will I offer My blood on an altar on the earth. 5 And as you petitioned for forgiveness through that blood, so also will I make My blood forgiveness of sins, and erase transgressions in it. 6 And now, behold, I have accepted your offering, O Adam, but the days of the covenant in which I have bound you are not fulfilled. When they are fulfilled, then will I bring you back into the garden. 7 Now, therefore, strengthen your heart; and when sorrow comes over you, make Me an offering, and I will be favorable to you".*

Although God accepted the first offering Adam made to Him in the form of Adam's own blood after he almost killed himself, God then forbade Adam to ever try to kill himself (First Book of Adam and Eve 25:1). Nevertheless, the first offering that Adam made to God became a custom for generations to come (First Book of Adam and Eve 25:7), not only for human beings, but for God Himself who ended offering himself at the cross to redeem the world, therefore making God consistent with how He started forgiving since the days of Adam and Eve until the end of the world. For God never changes.

As the story continues, Adam kept begging God to bring him back to the Garden, but God could not because He (God) cannot alter his covenant that had gone out of His mouth, hence Adam and Eve were told to be patient until the fulfillment of days (First Book of Adam and Eve 26:11-16). Although at times, Satan tried to kill Adam and Eve so that the Earth could belong to Satan and his hosts alone (First Book of Adam and Eve 28:8-10), God always had mercy on Adam and Eve and preserved them.

9.4. Adam begged for a gift from the Garden and God gave him a prophetic gift of gold, incense, and myrrh alluding to the kingdom, divinity, and death of Jesus Christ

As he mourned his loss of the Garden of Eden, Adam asked God to offer him something from the Garden as a token to him (First Book of Adam and Eve 29:5-8). Upon that request, God gave him golden rods, incense, and myrrh. Then, God told him:

Chapter 30:1 "... *God commanded the angel Gabriel to go down to the garden, and say to the cherub who kept it, "Behold, God has commanded me to come into the garden, and to take from it sweet smelling incense, and give it to Adam." 2 Then the angel Gabriel went down by God's order to the garden, and told the cherub as God had commanded him. 3 The cherub then said, "Well." And Gabriel went in and took the incense. 4 Then God commanded his angel Raphael to go down to the garden, and speak to the cherub about some myrrh, to give to Adam. 5 And the angel Raphael went down and told the cherub as God had commanded him, and the cherub said, "Well." Then Raphael went in and took the myrrh. 6 The golden rods were from the Indian sea, where there are precious stones. The incense was from the eastern border of the garden; and the myrrh from the western border, from where bitterness came over Adam. 7 And the angels brought these things to God by the Tree of Life in the garden. 8 Then God said to the angels, "Dip them in the spring of water; then take them and sprinkle their water over Adam and Eve, that they be a little comforted in their sorrow, and give them to Adam and Eve. 9 And the angels did as God had commanded them, and they gave all those things to Adam and Eve on the top of the mountain on which Satan had placed them, when he sought to make an end of them. 10* **And when Adam saw the golden rods, the incense, and the myrrh, he was rejoiced and cried because he thought that the gold was a token of the kingdom from where he had come, that the incense was a token of the bright light which had been taken from him, and that the myrrh was a token of the sorrow in which he was**" (First Book of Adam and Eve 30:1-12).

CHAPTER 9: COVENANT TO REDEEM ADAM, EVE, AND THEIR OFFSPRING

As the story continued into the next chapter, some translations such as that of Joseph Lumpkin mentioned an angel called "Suriyel" that other versions rendered as "Sahariel" in Chapter 31:5-6, a name that seems to have the same root as "Sahara" the name of the massive desert in Africa. I wondered whether some fallen angels could have been "buried" by God in the Sahara Desert.

9.5. God told Adam that rest can only be found in heaven, not on earth

With the suffering they were going through, Adam and Eve begged God at many times for rest. God had to answer them that they needed to live through the suffering of the moment until the world ends before rest could be given to their soul again. God also planned for the coming of Jesus to save the world first. For this world is not made to rest:

Chapter 42:1 *"Then came the Word of God to Adam, and said to him:—2 "O Adam, as to what you said, 'Bring me into a land where there is rest,' it is not another land than this, but it is the kingdom of heaven where alone there is rest. 3 But you can not make your entrance into it at present; but only after your judgment is past and fulfilled. 4 Then will I make you go up into the kingdom of heaven, you and your righteous descendants; and I will give you and them the rest you ask for at present. 5 And if you said, 'Give me of the Water of Life that I may drink and live'—it cannot be this day, but on the day that I shall descend into hell, and break the gates of brass, and bruise in pieces the kingdoms of iron. 6 Then will I in mercy save your soul and the souls of the righteous, to give them rest in My garden. And that shall be when the end of the world is come. 7 And, again, in regards to the Water of Life you seek, it will not be granted you this day; but on the day that I shall shed My blood on your head in the land that shall be called Golgotha. 8 For My blood shall be the Water of Life to you at that time, and not to just you alone, but to all your descendants who shall believe in Me; that it be to them for rest forever"* (First Book of Adam and Eve 42:1-8).

The Jewish culture teaches that Adam was buried in Golgotha, a site outside of Jerusalem's walls where Jesus was crucified, suggesting that the above prophecy given to Adam and Even really happened. Christian tradition places the tomb of Adam in Jerusalem under "Cave of Treasures", the place where Jesus was crucified. The Jewish tradition also believes that Adam and Eve's bodies were taken onto Noah's ark, and after the flood, were reburied in Jerusalem by Shem, the elder son of Noah. It is also believed that Shem and his great-grandson Eber moved to and started the City of Sem (giving the word Semites) or the city of Shem, which is now called Jerusalem.

God did not just promise Adam to redeem him and his obedient descendants one day, but He even told Adam when will that day be. In the Books of Adam and Eve, this date is encoded in the covenant of the great

ORIGIN OF THE SPIRITUAL WORLD

five and half days that God made with Adam. Indeed, as Adam and Eve cried out to God for mercy and to return to the Garden, God had pity on them and told them that He had made a covenant with them that He will not turn from, nor will let them return to the Garden until His *"covenant or great five and half days is fulfilled"* (First Book of Adam and Eve 7:1-3). I did not know what that great five and half days meant, but it may be an allusion to the 6 thousand years that will occur before the beginning of the Reign of Jesus on Earth for a 1000 year. Maybe, Adam had already lived for a half day before this event occurred, hence God talked about 5 and half days instead of 6 days.

CHAPTER 9: COVENANT TO REDEEM ADAM, EVE, AND THEIR OFFSPRING

Another Book by Nathanael-Israel Israel:
TURBULENT ORIGIN OF CHEMICAL PARTICLES

FIND ALL THE RELIABLE, CONVINCING, SCIENTIFIC ANSWERS YOU NEED TO SUCCESSFULLY DECODE THE ORIGIN OF CHEMICAL PARTICLES SAFELY

Where did all elementary particles and composite particles including atoms, molecules, minerals, and rocks come from? What are the fundamental factors, the machinery, and the generic processes that defined their formation and proprieties? What was the nature of their precursors at the beginning of the universe and what underlying processes shaped or molded them into the chemicals we know today? What was the primary cause of the abundance and diversity of chemicals in the celestial bodies in the universe? What is the accurate link between the formation of chemical particles and the formation of galaxies, stars, planets, asteroids, and satellites? What light can the origin of chemicals shed on the real cause and meaning of gravity and the other so-called fundamental forces in nature? How does the formation of the chemical particles fit into the big picture of the formation of the universe?

After studying these questions for more than 12 years, Dr. Nathanael-Israel Israel discovered that the proper understanding of the origin of chemical particles is a very challenging but profitable task that requires original, scientific, mathematic, and philosophic efforts beyond the current state of modern science—until recently. The solution for all of these puzzling problems: *"Turbulent Origin of Chemical Particles"*, the straightforward and trustworthy book that will help you to quickly, cheaply, easily, and efficiently navigate everything you need to know to finally solve the hard problems about the origin, the formation, and the functioning of all chemical particles. Whether you are a chemist, a biochemist, any other scientist, an engineer, as long as you have a reasonable background in chemistry but ignore how to scientifically demonstrate the origin of all chemical particles, this marvelous book is for you!

Amazingly packed with eye-popping analysis, fantastic graphs, tables, and the historic formula that broke the universe-origin code, *"Turbulent Origin of Chemical Particles"* will:

- Make it easier than ever for you to properly understand, decrypt, and articulate the real origin of natural chemical particles in the universe, therefore freeing you from false and boring explanations of the origin of all matters, and embrace the proven theory that opens doors to unparallel opportunities

- Professionally teach you how to transform the true knowledge of the origin of chemical particles into insights that significantly add value to your life in less time, and successfully establish you as a symbol of freedom, power, creativity, and originality in your field of expertise
- Fire you up to become the best version of you, and to cause positive changes to your initiatives that will profit you nonstop
- Discover thrilling illustrations and unconventional explanations of the formation of all matter in the universe, written in a simple language that brings humankind much closer to the complete deciphering of the mysteries at the very heart of chemistry, and open the way to a future of technology, innovation, discoveries, and breakthroughs
- Equip you to bypass technical knowledge that restricts non-experts from accessing the origin-related secrets contained in the massive scientific data, and get to the bottom of origin-related mysteries regardless of your background so you can empower yourself to leave unforgettable marks in your field of expertise
- Learn more at Science180.com/chemical

With *"Turbulent Origin of Chemical Particles"*, the accurate decrypting and understanding of the formation of chemicals has never been profitable and easy. Hence this great book is THE ultimate how-to guide for great people wanting to correctly decode the origin of the chemicals and positively transform their lives. Get this celebrated book today. Don't wait!

Known as the nonconformist, rule-breaker, and accurate demonstrator of the universe-origin, **Dr. Nathanael-Israel Israel** is the founder of Science180, the one-stop for answering the most crucial universe and life's origin questions. He has had the honor to be acknowledged as the fearless universe-origin decryption trailblazer. Learn more at Israel120.com.

CHAPTER 10

UNEARTH THE AMAZING STORY BEHIND THE FORMATION OF TIME, ETERNITY, AND END OF THE UNIVERSE (AND WHAT YOU CAN DO TO LIVE HAPPILY FOREVER)

What is time, and why did God (who lives in eternity) create it? In this chapter, I will introduce you to the mysterious significance of time and eternity. I have an incoming book devoted to time, and here, I will just present some pseudepigraphic mysteries about time.

10.1. Why did God create time and eternity?

One of the hot topics in science is time. Its meaning, origin, and management have been extensively studied, but the mystery surrounding it is still not fully unraveled yet. For some people, time is money. In contrast, science has put less emphasis on eternity. Religion is a field where eternity is most often discussed and believed. With the plurality of religion and scientific schools of thought, no clear consensus is found concerning time and eternity.

According to Enoch, God created time to allow men to reflect on it, count their deeds, ensure they observe God's laws, and meditate on their sins. God created eternity to be a reward for the believers and a punishment for unbelievers. For, at the end of time, the universe will be destroyed and replaced by a new world. Between the end of the current world and the beginning of eternity is the day of the Great Judgment:

2 Enoch 65:1 *And Enoch said to all his people: "... He [God] created man in the likeness of His own form, and put eyes into him to see, and ears into him to hear, and a heart to reflect, and intellect to enable him to deliberate. 3 And the Lord saw all the works of man, and created all his creatures, and divided time. From time he determined the years, and from the years he appointed the months, and from the months he appointed the days,*

and of days he appointed seven. 4 And in those he appointed the hours, measured them out exactly, that man might reflect on time and count years, months, and hours, as they alternate from beginning to end, so that he might count his own life from the beginning until death, and reflect on his sin and write his works, both bad and good. No work is hidden from the Lord, so that every man might know his works and never transgress all his commandments and keep My writing from generation to generation. 5 When all creation, both physical and spiritual, as the Lord created it, shall end, then every man goes to the great judgment, and then all-time shall be destroyed along with the years. And from then on, there will be neither months nor days nor hours. They will run together and will not be counted. 6 There will be one eon (age), and all the righteous who shall escape the Lord's great judgment, shall be collected in the great eon (age). For the righteous the great eon will begin, and they will live eternally, and there will be no labor, nor sickness, nor humiliation, nor anxiety, nor need, nor brutality, nor night, nor darkness, but great light among them. 7 And they shall have a great indestructible wall, and a paradise that is bright and eternal, for all mortal things shall pass away, and there will be eternal life.

According to the Bible, those who will not be saved will spend eternity in hell, whereas the saved will stay with God forever and ever in paradise. By the beginning of eternity, Enoch revealed that time will be destroyed as well as all mortal things, confirming the biblical account of the End Time. For instance, Apostle Paul and Peter in the Bible also mentioned that the world will end one day and that God will destroy the world with fire. Apostle John in the Book of Revelation (also called Apocalypse) also had a vision of the end time and the collapse of the world.

As Enoch was wrapping up his account of eternity, while encouraging his children to live a pure life, he told them that, in paradise, the just will shine more than the Sun sevenfold:

2 Enoch 66:6 For the Lord created all things. Bow not down to things made by man, leaving the Lord of all creation, because no work can remain hidden before the Lord's face. 7 Walk, my children, in long-suffering, in meekness, honesty, in thoughtfulness, in grief, in faith and in truth. Walk in (rely on) promises, in (times of) illness, in abuse, in wounds, in temptation, in nakedness, in privation, loving one another, until you go out from this age of ills, that you become inheritors of endless time. 8 **Blessed are the just who shall escape the great judgment, for they shall shine forth more than the sun sevenfold**, *for in this world the seventh part is taken off from all, light, darkness, food, enjoyment, sorrow, paradise, torture, fire, frost, and other things; he put all down in writing, that you might read and understand.*

This verse also suggests that the darkness of hell will be 7 times darker than the current darkness on earth. If the just will shine sevenfold than the Sun, it means that something must be preventing the Sun from shining more than it is now. That can also imply that matters in the Sun are not at their full brightness because of how their precursors were modified during the formation of the Sun. Similarly, the current darkness on Earth is not the darkest darkness, maybe because it is surrounded by light coming from stars

CHAPTER 10: TIME, ETERNITY, AND END OF THE UNIVERSE

in the night. Even at midnight when the Sun cannot be seen, stars shine some light onto the dark sky. However, when all bodies in the sky will be destroyed and hell will be completely separated from paradise (the dwelling of the just) the darkness of hell must be much darker than any current darkness on Earth. For instance, when Moses was performing miracles, signs, and wonders before Pharaoh in Egypt so he would free the Israelites from captivity, the Egyptians felt a thick darkness for three days, while the children of Israel had light in their dwelling (Exodus 10:21-23). This account confirms that there are levels of darkness.

Similarly, no enjoyment in this world is as much as that to come in heaven. In contrast, the pain unbelievers will suffer in hell is 7-fold worse than any current pain on earth. All of us must be careful in the choices we are making in this life so that in the last days, we don't see ourself with those who have rejected God, the Creator of all things who is "hiding" His face from human beings for now, but not forever. For the day is coming when everything will be clearly revealed, judgment made and rewards given. Are you ready?

10.2. Angels control the days and seasons

According to the Slavonic Book of Enoch, the seasons and the days of the years are controlled by angels, which respect their posts and duties. The following account of the division of the year according to the hierarchy of their leaders may be hiding a code of how celestial bodies are controlled by different forces and sources of power or motion (1 Enoch 82:10-20):

10 Their four leaders who divide the four parts of the year enter first; and after them the twelve leaders of the orders who divide the months; and for the three hundred and sixty days, there are heads over thousands who divide the days; and for the four days in the calendar there are the leaders which divide the four parts of the year. 11 And these heads over thousands are interspersed between leader and leader, each behind a station, but their leaders make the division. 12 And these are the names of the leaders who divide the four parts of the year which are ordained: 13 Milki'el, Hel'emmelek, and Mel'ejal, and Narel. And the names of those who lead them: Adnar'el, and Ijasusa'el, and 'Elome'el. 14 These three follow the leaders of the orders, and there is one that follows the three leaders of the orders which follow those leaders of stations that divide the four parts of the year. In the beginning of the year Melkejal rises first and rules, who is named Tam'aini and sun, and all the days of his dominion while he bears rule are ninety-one days. 15 And these are the signs of the days which are to be seen on earth in the days of his dominion: sweat, and heat; and calms; and all the trees bear fruit, and leaves are produced on all the trees, and the harvest of wheat, and the rose-flowers, and all the flowers which come out in the field, but the trees of the winter season become withered. 16 And these are the names of the leaders which are under them: Berka'el, Zelebs'el, and another who is added a head of a thousand, called Hilujaseph: and the days of the dominion of this leader are at an end. 17 The next leader after him is Hel'emmelek, whom one names the shining sun, and all the days of his light are ninety-one days. 18 And these are the signs of his days on the earth: glowing heat and dryness, and the trees ripen their fruits and produce all their fruits ripe and ready, and the sheep pair and become pregnant, and all the fruits of the earth are gathered in, and everything that is in the fields, and the winepress: these things take place in the days of his dominion. 19 These are the names, and the orders, and the leaders of those heads of thousands: Gida'ljal, Ke'el, and He'el, and the name of the head of a thousand which is added to them, Asfa'el: and the days of his dominion are at an end.

Here the beginning of the year mentioned in verse 14 should not be confounded with January, for the Jewish calendar counts days differently than the secular/Gregorian calendar. Most Jewish rituals go by the ecclesiastical calendar and the civil calendar. The beginning of the ecclesiastical year is Nissan (around end of March and beginning of April), whereas the Jewish civil calendar goes from Tishiri (around September-October). According to Jews, the civil calendar marks the beginning of creation, whereas the ecclesiastical calendar marks the reference for religious rituals.

10.5. Orbital parameters of the Moon and the Earth will change while the Sun will become brighter in the last days

Time on Earth is mostly measured by referring to the Sun, the Moon, and the Earth one way or the other. However, the movement of these celestial bodies can be altered, therefore significantly changing a lot of things. For instance, 1 Enoch 80 contains some deep secrets about the relationship between Earth speed and Sun brightness in the last days:

1 Enoch 80:*2 And in the days of the sinners the years shall be shortened, and their seed shall be tardy on their lands and fields, and* **all things on the earth shall alter, and shall not appear in their time**. *And the rain shall be kept back, and heaven shall withhold it. 3 And in those times the fruits of the earth shall be backward, and shall not* **grow in their time, and the fruits of the trees shall be withheld in their time. 4 And the moon shall alter her customs, and not appear at her time**. *5 And in those days* **the sun shall be seen and he shall journey in the evening on the extremity of the great chariot in the west and shall shine** *more brightly than accords with the order of light.*

In the last days, the orbital parameters of celestial bodies including the Moon and the Earth will be altered. The increase of the brightness of the Sun implies that its chemical composition and/or its orbital parameters may change as well and/or that the distance between the Earth and the Sun will be reduced. These changes that will occur with the Moon, Earth, and the Sun suggest that their current characteristics are connected by a law, which is alterable.

God can alter or reverse the movement of anything if He wishes. Similarly, those who believe in God can pray to Him to stop the motion of some celestial bodies and it can happen. For instance, Joshua (the successor of Moses) prayed and the Moon and the Sun stood still for hours: *"And the*

CHAPTER 10: TIME, ETERNITY, AND END OF THE UNIVERSE

sun stood still, and the moon stayed, until the people had avenged themselves upon their enemies. Is not this written in the book of Jasher? So the sun stood still in the midst of heaven, and hasted not to go down about a whole day" (Joshua 10:13). Like the verses you just read said, that story about Joshua is also recounted not only in the Bible but also in the Book of Jasher 88:63-65. But did you ever wonder why that Book of Jasher itself is not in the Bible? If the Book of Jasher is worth mentioning in the Bible, you should read it. For I believe that the books mentioned in the Bible are worth reading such as the Book of Jasher, the Books of Enoch, and the book of Jubilees. If the men of God who wrote the Bible referenced such books, who are we to reject them? Because the great men of God who transcribed the Bible valued those books, we too should do the same.

10.3. The world will likely end before it is 8,000 years old

At the beginning of the 8th millennium since creation, eternity will begin, confirming that the Earth will be destroyed by that time:

2 Enoch 33:1 And I appointed the eighth day also, that the eighth day should be the first-created after my work, and that the first seven revolve in the form of the seventh thousand, and that **at the beginning of the eighth thousand there should be a time of not-counting, endless, with neither years nor months nor weeks nor days nor hours.**

This assertion confirms some biblical interpretations according to which God will return to earth 6000 years after its creation, then rule from Israel as the King of the whole Earth for 1000 years before eternity begins (Bible's Book of Revelation 19-20).

2 Enoch 33:2 ... **there is no counselor nor inheritor to my creations. 3 I am eternal unto myself, not made with hands, and without change. 4 My thought is my own counselor, my wisdom and my word create***, and my eyes observe how all things stand here and tremble with terror. 5* **If I turn away my face, then all things will be destroyed.**

All it will take for God to destroy creation is turn His face, implying that the seating of God on His throne sustains the creatures. In other words, the world is still connected to God who can change its course any time He wants. For God has been watching over His creatures so that in the end, they "fulfill His plan". Those who refuse to believe in God and give Him the praise He deserves are just ignorant of the foundations and laws that created the universe. Oh God! Receive my worship and praise for Your designing and creating the world so perfectly harmonized with Your eternal purpose!

10.4. Destruction or collapse of the universe

No book has clearly presented what the end of the world will look like. The Bible detailed what will happen before the return of Jesus Christ, but not a whole lot about how the world will be destroyed or how God will recreate a new heaven and a new earth. The vision that Enoch had about the destruction of the Earth and probably the collapse of the universe that he recounted to his son, Methuselah, shines some light on the issue (1 Enoch 83:2-7):

2 I [Enoch] saw two visions before I got married (took a wife), and the one was quite unlike the other: the first when I was learning to write: the second before I married (took) your mother, was when I saw a terrible vision. 3 And regarding them I prayed to the Lord. I had laid down in the house of my grandfather Mahalalel, when **I saw in a vision how heaven collapsed and was carried off (removed, torn down) and fell to the earth. 4 And when it fell to the earth, I saw how the earth was swallowed up in a great abyss, and mountains were suspended on mountains, and hills sank down on hills, and high trees were ripped from their stems, and hurled down and sunk in the abyss. 5 And then, a word fell into my mouth, and I lifted up my voice to cry aloud, and said: 6 'The earth is destroyed.'** *And my grandfather Mahalalel woke me as I lay near him and said to me: 'Why do you cry so, my son, and why do you make such moaning (lamentation)?' 7 And I recounted to him the whole vision which I had seen, and he said to me: 'You have seen a terrible thing, my son. Your dream (vision) is of a grave time and concerns the secrets of all the sin of the earth: it must sink into the abyss and be totally destroyed.'"*

The Bible's Book of Revelation also presents an account of the collapse of the universe as leaves falling from a fig tree (Revelation 6:12-14):

Revelation 6:12 "**I saw when the Lamb opened the sixth seal, and there was a great earthquake. The sun became as black as sackcloth made of goat's hair, and the full moon became like blood. 13 The stars of heaven fell to the earth like a fig tree drops unripe figs when shaken by a great wind. 14 The heaven ripped apart like a scroll being rolled up, and every mountain and island was moved from their places. 15 Then the kings of the earth and the great men and the military commanders and the rich and the mighty and everyone—slave and free—hid themselves in the caves and among the rocks of the mountains.** *16 And they tell the mountains and the rocks, 'Fall on us, and hide us from the face of the One seated on the throne and from the wrath of the Lamb. 17 For the great day of their wrath has come, and who is able to stand?"* (Tree of Life Version).

Honestly, I don't know if the aforementioned vision of Enoch and of Apostle John in the Book of Revelation are about the collapse of the whole world or not. Nevertheless, the information they convey points at some of the things that can happen during the end of the universe. While answering some watchers (fallen angels which sinned for instance by sleeping with women) who begged him to ask God to forgive them, Enoch also revealed that the heaven and the Earth will end one day forever:

2 Enoch 18:5 And I said to the Grigori: I saw your brethren and their works, and their great torments, and I prayed for them, but the Lord has condemned them (to be) **under earth till (the existing) heaven and earth shall end forever.**

CHAPTER 10: TIME, ETERNITY, AND END OF THE UNIVERSE

'Science180 Academy' Success Strategy:
SCIENCE180 MODELS OF THE ORIGIN OF THE UNIVERSE AND ITS CONTENT

Science180 Models consist of all the theories elaborated by Nathanael-Israel Israel regarding his ground breaking discovery on the origin of the universe and its content including all forms of life and chemical particles. These theories are detailed in various books written by Dr. Nathanael-Israel Israel encompass the following:

1. SCIENCE180 MODEL OF COSMOLOGY, also called Science180 Cosmology, Science180 Model of Cosmology, Science180 Cosmological Model, a scientific theory that explains Science180 to the scientists. Discover the details of this model in Nathanael-Israel Israel's book titled *"Turbulent Origin of the Universe"*. In that book, you will also unearth the new physics that will revolutionize science forever and land you into a zone of original ideas that improve lives nonstop regardless of your expertise.

2. SCIENCE180 CREATIONISM, also called Science180 Model of the Creation of the Universe and Life by God, a scientific theory that presents the origin of the universe in a biblical language. If you want to learn more about how to scientifically prove the Biblical account of the creation of the universe and the existence of God in a way that makes the head of God deniers to spin faster than a DJ's turntable, then get Nathanael-Israel Israel's book titled *"Reconciling Science and Creation Accurately"*.

3. SCIENCE180 MODEL OF THE ORIGIN OF CHEMICAL PARTICLES, a scientific theory that explains the origin of chemical particles with the perspective of Science180 Turbulence. If you want to professionally learn how to transform the true knowledge of the origin of chemical particles into insights that significantly add value to your life in less time, successfully establish you as a symbol of freedom, power, creativity, and originality in your field of expertise, get *"Turbulent Origin of Chemical Particles"*, THE ultimate how-to guide for great people wanting to correctly decode the origin of the chemicals and positively transform their lives. Get this celebrated book today. Don't wait!

4. SCIENCE180 MODEL FOR THE GENERAL PUBLIC (which explains the origin of the universe and life to the general public in a language that laypeople can understand). Find out more in Nathanael-Israel Israel's book called *"From Science to Bible's Conclusions"*, a scientifically verifiable, bestselling book to finally get the accurate, jaw-dropping answer that has been rationally shaking believers, skeptics, and freethinkers. Get this very popular book today.

5. SCIENCE180 MODEL OF LIFE-ORIGIN, or Science180 Model of the Origin of Life, a scientific theory that explains the origin of all forms of life using turbulence. To unlock the step-by-step pathway to decode the origin of life and get the power, freedom, and boldness to detect, correct, and remove all misinformation, ambiguity, and misleading claims and theories surrounding the life-origin and take advantage of the opportunities that an accurate understanding of the life-origin creates, get Nathanael-Israel Israel's book titled *"Turbulent Origin of Life"*.

6. SCIENCE180 MODEL FOR CHILDREN, a children's version of the theory of the origin of the universe and life in a language that 7-12 years old children can properly understand. To know the proven formula that helps children to easily answer their huge universe-origin and life-origin questions with confidence, humor, and joy, get *"How Baby Universe Was Born"*, the pragmatic book that has been causing children to belly laugh and thank those who offered it to them.

7. SCIENCE180 MODEL OF PSEUDEPIGRAPHA, a deep explanation of the secrets of the origin of the universe and life revealed a long time ago, but hidden from the general public. To discover how the only one ancient blueprint has the reliable power to help you to accurately decrypt the spiritual origin and history of everything in the universe, get *"Origin of the Spiritual World"*. In it, you will discover deep rejected secrets that have prevented humankind from unearthing the beginning of the universe and know how to properly use the lost and rejected scriptures to articulate the process by which the universe was formed, so you can use that insight to improve your understanding of the Bible, innovate in your domain of interest, and improve your life.

CHAPTER 10: TIME, ETERNITY, AND END OF THE UNIVERSE

8. *SCIENCE180 MODEL OF THE PROOF OF THE EXISTENCE OF GOD*, a theory that ties together most of Nathanael-Israel Israel's discoveries that scientifically prove the existence of God. With Nathanael-Israel Israel's book "*Science180 Accurate Scientific Proof of God*", you will surely know the only way to scientifically know if God exist, and if so, which of the thousands of beings worshipped across the globe is the true God. In that book, you will also discover the errors in the scientific and religious theories (about the origin of the universe, life, and chemicals) that are putting you at a high risk you will never recover from if you don't quickly and confidently learn how to rationally take control over threats lurking at the edge of your efforts to understand the universe and life today.

9. SCIENCE180 THEORY OF EVERYTHING, (also called the theory of all theories), ties together everything in the universe into a single theory. Checkout Science180.com to learn more about the incoming book that covers this extremely important topic.

CHAPTER 11

SEVEN SECRETS YOU IGNORE ABOUT THE JOURNEY OF ENOCH TO HEAVEN AND WHAT HE DID WHEN GOD COMMANDED HIM TO PUBLISH HEAVENLY SECRETS FOR THE BENEFIT OF HUMAN BEINGS

Unlike fallen angels who wrongly revealed heavenly secrets to human beings, Enoch wrote about creation secrets to human beings because God asked him to do so when he visited heaven. In this chapter, I will present how God instructed Enoch, and what are the circumstances surrounding his return from heaven after meeting God, what he prophesized about the discovery, spread, and witnessing about this book, particularly in the last days. In the process, I will explain how that fits into our big picture of the origin of the spiritual world.

11.1. God commissioned Enoch to publish what he saw in heaven

God asked Enoch to share with his children the things he saw in heaven. He commanded that the books of Enoch must be transmitted throughout generations. God did not intend that the books of Enoch be kept secret.

2 Enoch 33:6 Apply your mind, Enoch, and know him [God] *who is speaking to you, and take the books there, which you yourself have written. 7 I give you Samuil and Raguil, who led you upward with the books, and* **go down to earth, and tell your sons all that I have told you,** *and all that you have seen, from the lower heaven up to my throne, … 9* **Give them the books of the handwriting, and they will read them and will know that I am the creator of all things** *and will understand how there is no other God but me. 10* **And let them distribute the books of your handwriting from children to children, generation to generation, nation to nation.**

ORIGIN OF THE SPIRITUAL WORLD

When Enoch talked to his children about the books, he taught them to distribute them to their children, to all generations, and among the nations.

*2 Enoch 48:5 **So I teach you, my children, and tell you to distribute the books to your children, into all your generations, and among the nations who shall have the sense to fear God.*** *Let them receive them, and may they come to love them more than any food or earthly sweets and read them and apply themselves to them. 6 And those who do not understand the Lord, who do not fear God, who do not accept, but reject, who do not receive the books, a terrible judgment awaits these.*

2 Enoch 54:1 Let these books, which I have given you, be for an inheritance of your peace in that time that you do not understand things. 2 Hand them to all who want them, and instruct them, that they may see the Lord's very great and marvelous works.

In addition to the books that bear his name, Enoch is also the author of the Book of Adam and Eve, which I also quote a lot in this book. Without reading the Books of Enoch, it would be hard or impossible to know the author of the Book of Adam and Eve. Indeed, in the Books of Enoch, it is said that God commanded Enoch to write the Book of Adam. Enoch wrote that pseudepigrapha under the guidance of Archangel Michael:

2 Enoch 33:11 And Enoch, I [God] will give you, my intercessor, the archangel Michael, for the writings of your fathers Adam, Seth, Enos, Cainan, Mahaleleel, and Jared your father.

That book which I also read gives a deep insight into the life of Adam, Eve, and their children. It deeply counts the fall of humankind and its immediate consequence. Unfortunately, not only have the Books of Enoch been rejected by many people, but those who discovered them hid them. One thing I have realized is that, just as God cannot be hidden, the truth about the world He created will not be rejected or hidden forever. God wishes His creative work be understood by the world, else He would not have revealed it in the first place. Because there is also a time for each thing on Earth, I believe that God has set this time aside for me to scientifically shine some light onto the scientific details of what God has done. In other words, just as God commissioned Enoch to publish what he saw in heaven, I felt commanded to scientifically explain the creation story in the Books of Enoch and in the Bible to human beings, and to impart human beings with the true knowledge that can profit them today and forever if they decide to follow God. As of today, very few Christians and Jews know the Books of Enoch. Most of those who know that the Books of Enoch exist don't believe it is authentic or don't take the time to properly read it. I have heard many people and even famous prophets confess the authenticity of the Books of Enoch, yet, they talk as if they are aware of their content, and consequently, they said things opposing them. Because most believers didn't read the Books of Enoch, the secrets God revealed to Enoch have been unknown by most human beings. The rejection of those secrets by human beings can also be part of God's plan for, as I explained in other books, if some human beings

CHAPTER 11: GOD COMMANDED ENOCH TO PUBLISH HEAVENLY SECRETS OF CREATION

had understood those secrets since the time of Enoch, they could have "scientifically" misused some of them to destroy one another and even the earth long ago. Therefore, I marvel at God's infinite wisdom and grace.

11.2. Enoch's face was frozen before he left heaven to return to earth

After Enoch finished his visit to heaven, God asked an angel to freeze his face, otherwise, no one on earth could behold it.

2 Enoch 37:1 And the Lord called upon one of the older angels, terrible and menacing, and placed him by me, in appearance white as snow, and his hands like ice, having the appearance of great frost, and he froze my face, because I could not endure the terror of the Lord, just as it is not possible to endure a stove's fire and the sun's heat, and the frost of the air. 2 And the Lord said to me: Enoch, if your face be not frozen here, no man will be able to behold your face.

If God had not frozen Enoch's face, it could have killed people for it was full with God's glory and energy. This story is similar to what happened to Moses' face after he met God at Mount Sinai. The Bible recounts that Moses' face was shining and it needed to be covered. Surely, after their fall, Adam and Eve lost God's glory that was on them. For they were in constant contact with heaven and heavenly beings before their fall. In other words, like I said in other chapters, Adam and Eve were originally full with God's glory, but they lost it because of sin. According to 3 Enoch 5:1, God removed His glory (*Shekina*) from earth during the time of Enosh (who is different from Enoch) because of the increase of sins, particularly idolatry (*3 Enoch 5:1*). Enosh was a descent of Seth and he became the head of all idol worshippers of the world (3 Enoch 5:6). God was angry at human worship of idols and His glory could no longer dwell on earth. Until today, one of the things God hates the most is idolatry. For He alone deserves to be worshipped and praised. The loss of the glory may have also led human beings to start looking for things to cloth themselves, cover their shame, nudity, and vulnerability after their fall. I elaborated on that in others incoming books particularly those related to the domination and fall of man. The glory of God wrapped the whole world at the beginning (3 Enoch 5:4). The Shekinah (the glory of the divine presence) enfolded the world from end to end and protected human beings from sickness and demonic attacks. After the fall of Adam and Eve, the Shekina (Glory) would have stayed in the Garden of Eden for a while before God removed it from the Earth:

3 Enoch 5:(1) **From the day when the Holy One, blessed be He, evicted the first Adam from the Garden of Eden, and continuing from that day, the Shekina (glory) was dwelling upon a Cherub under the Tree of Life ... (3) And the first man and his children were sitting outside the gate of the Garden to see the glowing, bright appearance of the Shekina (glory). (4) For the splendor of the Shekina (glory) enfolds the world from end to end** *with its splendor 365,000 times that of the orb of the sun. And everyone who made use of the splendor of the Shekina, on him no flies and no gnats lit, and he was not ill and he suffered no pain. No demons could overpower him, neither were they able to injure him. (5) When the Holy One, blessed be He, went out and went in from the Garden to Eden, ... then everything and everyone saw His magnificent Shekina and they were not injured; (6) until the time of the generation of Enosh who was the head of all idol worshippers of the world.*

These verses suggest that the conditions on Earth at the beginning of the world were different than those of today. Scientific data proves that the conditions on Earth, including the climate, are changing. The presence of the Shekina on Earth could be one of the reasons people had a very high lifespan before the Noah flood. For instance, Adam lived for 930 years. It was after the flood that human lifespan was reduced to 120 years. Despite medical progress, human lifespan is still significantly reduced and very few people reach 120 years before dying, confirming that conditions on Earth have really been worsening.

11.3. Under God's permission, Enoch revealed creation secrets to Moses at Mount Sinai

According to 3 Enoch 48-D, Enoch taught heavenly secrets to Moses at Mount Sinai. Let's not forget that when God gave the Ten Commandment to Moses, he spent 40 days and nights on the mountain. The Hebrew Book of Enoch revealed that it was during that period that Enoch taught Moses deep secrets about creation. This may explain why the story of Enoch correlates with that of the Bible's Book of Genesis

When Enoch revealed these secrets to Moses, some of the angels were enraged against him. Despite him explaining to them that he did so because God gave him permission and authority, some angels did not stop arguing. Therefore, God scorned them and drove them away from Him with contempt, suggesting that some angels may have fallen after the giving of the laws to Moses.

3 Enoch 48 – D(1) Seventy names has Metatron [Enoch] *which the Holy One, blessed be He, took from His own name and put upon him* [Enoch]. *And these are .... Segansakkiel, the Prince of Wisdom. (2) And why is he called by the name Sagnesakiel? Because* **all the storehouses of wisdom are committed in to his hand. (3) And all of them were opened to Moses on Sinai, so that he learned them during the forty days, while he remained.** *He learned the Torah in the seventy ways it applies to the seventy nations, ... (4) But as soon as the forty days were completed, he* [Moses] *forgot all of them in one moment. Then the Holy One, blessed be He, called Yephiphyah, the Prince of the Law, and (through him) they were given to Moses as a gift, for it is written (Deut. 10:4): "and the Lord gave them to me* [Moses]*." And after that it remained with him. And how do we know that it remained in his memory? Because it is*

CHAPTER 11: GOD COMMANDED ENOCH TO PUBLISH HEAVENLY SECRETS OF CREATION

written (Mal. 55: 4): "Remember the Law of Moses my servant which I commanded unto him in Horeb for all Israel, even my statues and judgments." 'The Law of Moses': that is the Torah, the Prophets and the Writings, ... And all of them were given to Moses on high on Sinai ... (7) **"YHWH, the God of Israel, is my witness that I [Enoch] revealed this secret to Moses and when I did all the host all the high heavens were enraged against me. (8) They asked me, saying, "Why do you reveal this secret to a son of man, born of woman, who is tainted and unclean, a man of the putrefying drop? You gave him the secret by which heaven and earth, sea and land, mountains and hills, rivers and springs, Gehenna of fire and hail, the Garden of Eden and the Tree of Life were all created and by which Adam and Eve, and the cattle, and the wild beasts, the birds of the air, and the fish of the sea, and Behemoth and Leviathan, and the crawling things, the snakes, the dragons of the sea, and the creeping things of the deserts; and Torah and Wisdom and Knowledge and Thought and the imparted knowledge and the Gnosis of things above and of heaven and the fear of heaven were all created. Why did you reveal this to flesh and blood? I answered them: Because the Holy One, blessed be He, has given me authority. And furthermore, I have obtained permission from the high and exalted throne, from which all the explicit names go forth with lightning and fire and flaming chashrnallim. (9) But they (the hosts) were not appeased or satisfied, until the Holy One, blessed be He, scorned them and drove them away from Him with contempt and said to them: "I delight in him [Enoch], and have set my love on him, and have entrusted to him and given unto Metatron [Enoch], my Servant, and I have given to him alone, for he [Enoch] is Unique among all the children of heaven. (10) And Metatron brought them out from his house and storehouses and gave these secrets to Moses, and Moses gave them to Joshua, and Joshua gave them to the elders, and the elders gave them the prophets and the men of the Great Synagogue, and the men of the Great Synagogue gave them to Ezra and Ezra the Scribe gave them to Hillel the elder,** and Hillel the elder gave them to Rabbi Abbahu and Rabbi Abbahu to Rabbi Zera, and Rabbi Zera to the men of faith, and the men of faith gave them to give warning and to heal by them all disease that ravaged the world."

I thank God for allowing me to discover these precious Books of Enoch without which I may have made a major universal mistake in my perspective of the formation of the universe. I hope the readers of this book will be motivated to believe and follow God the Father and His Only Begotten Son, Jesus Christ, and the Holy Spirit the rest of their life.

11.4. Enoch's prophecy about the discovery of his books
Enoch prophesied that his books will be given to wise people in the last days by wise men who will witness to the children of the Earth is those days:
1 Enoch 104:12 Then, I [Enoch] know another mystery, that books will be given to the

righteous and the wise to produce joy and righteousness and much wisdom. 13 And **to them the books shall be given, and they shall believe them and rejoice over them, and then all the righteous who have learned from them all the paths of righteousness shall be paid back.**
1 Enoch 105:1 **In those days, the Lord called them (the wise and righteous) to testify to the children of earth concerning their wisdom: Show it to them; for you are their guides, and a recompense over the whole earth.** *2 For I [God] and my son will be united with them forever in the paths of righteousness in their lives; and you shall have peace: rejoice, you children of righteousness. Amen.*

I thank God Almighty, and I believe I am one of the wise men that Enoch prophesied would discover his books and testify of them before the world. Hence, God is using me mightily to guide the scientists and nonscientists through the discovery and understanding of creation based on the wisdom of Enoch, who, since God took him, is not among the dead, but is living in heaven, and who, according to the Hebrew Book of Enoch, is above all angels, and who, to my understanding, is positioned right now as the third person in heaven after God the Father and God the Son.

11.5. Spiritual beings do not need physical food or earthly enjoyment

Enoch spent 60 days in heaven, then he was sent back to earth where he stayed for 30 days before the holy angels took him indefinitely to heaven where he now lives (2 Enoch 36) as the Metatron above the angels. Beforehand, Enoch gave his children his last words during his last 30 days on Earth. During that short 30-day stay, he revealed to them that he ate no food while he was in heaven and that he was not hungry. The transformation Enoch went through after God asked an angel to anoint him with ointment of His [God's] glory and replace his earthly garments would have been the reason he was not hungry. During his 30 days on earth, Enoch did not eat either. For, unlike earthly matter, heavenly materials are perfect, incorruptible, and immortal. As the angels of God were urging Enoch that his time on earth was up and that he needed to go back to heaven, the uppermost Jerusalem, he said his last words to his children:

2 Enoch 55:1 My children, behold, the day of my determined period (term and time) has approached. 2 For the angels who shall go with me are standing before me and urge me to my departure from you. They are standing here on earth, awaiting what has been told them. 3 For tomorrow I shall go up to heaven, to the uppermost Jerusalem, to my eternal inheritance. 4 Therefore I bid you to do the Lord's good pleasure before his face at all times.
2 Enoch 56:1 Methuselah answered his father Enoch, and said: What (food) is agreeable to your eyes, father, that I may prepare before your face, that you may bless our houses, and your sons, and that your people may be made glorious through you, and then that you may depart, as the Lord said?" **2 Enoch answered his son Methuselah and said: "Hear me, my child. From the time when the Lord anointed me with the**

CHAPTER 11: GOD COMMANDED ENOCH TO PUBLISH HEAVENLY SECRETS OF CREATION

ointment of his glory, there has been no food in me, and my soul remembers not earthly enjoyment, neither do I want anything earthly."

This statement proved that spiritual beings don't need earthly food as they are made of the highest materials that resist the degradation constraints of the Earth, which is limited. Living organisms including human beings have needs on Earth because they are made of ingredients that are in constant movement and subject to degradation, etc. Hence, a need to replenish them or do something so they can stay in some equilibrium with one another. For instance, living organisms have to eat to replenish their energy, whereas nonliving things move to balance energy or maintain their states, their constitution and other characteristics related to their nature.

If God had formed a lot of chemical elements of earth, life may have been harder for it could take more energy and efforts to satisfy the laws that sustain more elements than a few elements. Similarly, if less chemical elements existed on Earth, life would have been different and the biochemical needs might have been met with different types and amounts of effort. Surely, chemistry on Earth is in harmony with human needs. I provided more details in my books *"Turbulent Origin of Chemical Particles"* and *"Turbulent Origin of Life"*.

11.6. How Enoch was taken to heaven at the end of his life on Earth

After his journey to heaven, Enoch was given a few more days before he was taken to be with God indefinitely. When the time for God to take Enoch came, the Earth was covered with darkness, and the angels took him to be in the presence of God.

2 Enoch 67:1 When Enoch had talked to the people, the Lord sent out darkness on to the earth, and there was darkness, and it covered those men standing with Enoch, and they took Enoch up on to the highest heaven, where the Lord is. And there, God received him and placed him before His face, and the darkness went off from the earth, and light came again. 2 And the people saw and did not understand how Enoch had been taken, and they glorified God, and found a scroll in which was written "The God of the Spiritual." Then all went to their dwelling places.

As a reminder, when Jesus Christ was dying at the cross, the Earth was also covered in darkness, suggesting that the death of Jesus and the rapture of Enoch may have something in common. After Enoch was taken to heaven, his children celebrated and praised God for giving them a sign through him.

2 Enoch 68:1 Enoch was born on the sixth day of the month Tsivan (the first month of the year) and lived three hundred and sixty-five years. 2 He was taken up to heaven on the first day of the month Tsivan **and remained in heaven sixty days.** *3 He wrote all these signs of all creation, which the Lord created, and wrote three hundred and sixty-six books, and handed them over to his sons and* **remained on earth thirty days and was again taken up to heaven** *on the sixth day of the month Tsivan, on the very day* *and hour when he was born. ... 6 Methuselah and his brethren,* **all the sons of Enoch, made haste, and erected an altar at that place called Achuzan, where Enoch had been taken up to heaven. 7 And they took sacrificial oxen and summoned all people and sacrificed the sacrifice before the Lord's face. 8 All people,** *the elders of the people and the whole assembly came to the feast and brought gifts to the sons of Enoch. 9 And they made a great feast, rejoicing and making merry three days, praising God, who had given them such a sign through Enoch, who had found favor with him, and that they should hand it on to their sons from generation to generation, from age to age. Amen.*

11.7. Why did God remove Enoch from humankind?

The short answer is that God removed Enoch, a tribute from His world under all the heavens, from humankind to be a witness against the generation of Cain on the Day of Judgment. Indeed, God said that He took Enoch as a tribute to Himself, meaning that Enoch was the best specimen humankind had offered God (3 Enoch 6), because among the inhabitants of the world, Enoch is equal to all of them (put together) in his faith, righteousness, and perfection of deed. Consequently, when Enoch reached heaven, God treated him very well. Unfortunately, some angels were "jealous" at the treatment Enoch received when he joined heaven in such a way that God had to explain to them that Enoch is a special specimen:

3 Enoch 6 ... My servants, my host, my Cherubim, my Ophannim, my Seraphim! Do not be displeased on account of this. **Since all the children of men have denied me [God]** *and my great Kingdom and have all gone worshipping idols, I have removed my Shekina from among them and have lifted it up on high. But this one [Enoch] whom I have taken from among them is an Elect One among (the inhabitants of) the world and he is equal to all of them (put together) in his faith, righteousness and perfection of deed and I have taken him as a tribute from my world under all the heavens.*

According to the translator Joseph B. Lumpkin, *"the statement of 'taking a tribute' can be better understood if one looks at Enoch as the best mankind has to offer and God took him as an act of admiration indicating the intended worth of mankind, had they not turned away from Him"*. According to the story, God removed Enoch from the Earth to be a witness against the inhabitants of the world. In the book of Revelation (Apocalypse) chapter 11, the Bible speaks about two witnesses who will do supranatural miracles, signs, and wonders in the last days. Most commentators believe that these two witnesses are Enoch and Elijah.

When I was meditating on the admiration God has for Enoch and the special witness that he [Enoch] will give on the last days, I felt the Holy Spirit moving inside of me, causing me to do something to testify of who God is to the scientific community. Since then, I have always felt that God is still looking for witnesses to testify about Him to the world. I know that very soon, God has put me aside for Science180, to decode and explain Biblical

CHAPTER 11: GOD COMMANDED ENOCH TO PUBLISH HEAVENLY SECRETS OF CREATION

creation to the whole world for His glory.

'Science180 Academy' Success Strategy
SCIENCE180 PUBLISHING: AUTHORS WANTED

Science180 Publishing, the American publishing company that published the groundbreaking discovery about the origin of the universe, of life, and of chemicals spearheaded by Dr. Nathanael-Israel Israel, really wants to publish your book(s) regardless of your field of expertise. This is a unique opportunity for:

- established authors
- people aspiring to become authors
- people who have written a book or are wanting to write one and need help with anything regarding publishing
- people who are not well known, inexperienced
- people whose books are viewed as nonconformist, controversial, or unconventional
- people who do not have enough resources or knowledge to navigate the publishing process
- people who are struggling to find an affordable, experienced, and high-quality publisher

Although Science180 Publishing is based in the USA, it can publish your books within your budget regardless of your geographical location. Science180 Publishing is highly interested in your document and possibly helping you publish it. Please visit Science180Publishing.com to explore how we may assist you. No matter the content of your book, as far as it is original, not promoting anything illegal, not duplicating anyone else's idea, Science180 Publishing can help you publish it in the USA. Please contact us asap and see how we can help.

To start your journey of publishing your book with Science180 Publishing, please visit Science180Publishing.com today.

CHAPTER 12

THE SECRETS ABOUT THE ORIGIN OF THE UNIVERSE, LIFE, AND ANGELS HIDDEN IN THE REJECTED BOOKS—THAT YOU WON'T LEARN AT MOST CHURCHES—BECAUSE THEY DON'T WANT YOU TO KNOW OR THEY DON'T KNOW THEM

Although some people may claim that God did not reveal many details about the creation of the universe and everything in it, many lost or rejected books will refute that claim, for they contain a lot of information, which people have refused to pay attention to for thousands of years. Some of these lost or rejected books which contain key information on the formation of the universe include the Book of Jasher, the Book of Jubilees also cited in the Bible, Book of Esdras, the Book of Magdalena, the Books of Enoch, the Books of Adam and Eve, and many more. Fortunately, I found and read all of these books which are filled with a wealth of information that people have mistakenly discarded for so long. The Books of Enoch and the Books of Adam and Eve particularly interested me very much because they contain top information about creation and the life of the first human beings. These books abound with rich information sometimes difficult to digest for those who want to complicate their interpretation.

Enoch revealed many mysterious things after God commissioned angels to bring him to Heaven, where visions of the creation of the universe were given to him. One of the first things Enoch saw was "ether" in space, and I wonder if the misinterpretation of this information led to the writing of ether theories in the literature. The Books of Enoch also revealed that stars in the universe are ruled by angels and that the movement of the Sun for instance is

CHAPTER 12: CONCLUSION

associated with the blowing of winds and the effect of four stars, while the light of the Sun is kindled by angels. They also expounded of how God stretched or *spread forth heavens visible (physical) and invisible (spiritual). It also revealed how* stars and celestial bodies were formed from a fire. Winds are described as the pillar of the universe and they move stars and the moon. Likewise, winds surrounded the Earth and they are blown under the wings of angels.

The Sun and the Moon are bound together by an oath and one star in the universe is bigger than the others. Orbital parameters of the Moon and the Earth will change, while the Sun will become brighter in the last days. The Books of Enoch revealed a hierarchy among celestial bodies. Celestial bodies move in circular chariots according to their leaders. The Book of Enoch explained that when Enoch arrived at the 10th Heaven (called Aravat in Hebrew), he was transfigured before meeting God. There, God revealed to him that He created the physical world from the spiritual world. The first physical body created, Adoil, was fragmentated to birth precursors including a light God sent above His throne to be the foundation of things of high things. The story suggests that the breaking apart or fragmentation of Adoil was very noisy, powerful, and divided the original precursors into pieces. Adoil may have not been 100% light, but at least in its "belly" was a light. Belly could mean the interior or center of Adoil. This points to the fact that the exterior of Adoil may not have been light, but a material that may have been solid or dark. The existence of light in the belly of Adoil corroborates also the fact that most bodies are hotter on the inside than the outside.

The Slavonic Book of Enoch also revealed that God created His own throne, positioned his seat on it and commanded the created light to go above the throne. According to the story, the materials in Adoil were not initially hard, but at one-point God commanded it to harden and it was so. Additionally, the notion of weight and color was introduced as it is said that Archas came up heavy and very red. The material in Adoil may have gone through a process that made them to become the hard Archas. The opening of Archas and its giving birth to the lowest things implies that something happened after Archas was split into different bodies. The story suggests that, the first stage of the formation of the universe was the formation of a huge body which inside was full of fiery materials. Then that body was fragmentated to birth many pieces of bodies that were highly in light. The narrative illustrates how water was formed. It also provides details on the formation of the Earth including a process by which large rocks were piled up. This suggested to me that if rocks were not piled together, the precursor of the earth could have become a cluster of rocks moving together like the main belt asteroids. The Books of Enoch suggest that the hardening of celestial bodies appeared after their precursors were formed.

The lost and rejected scriptures (Pseudepigrapha) revealed many processes not mentioned or detailed in the Bible. These processes include for instance

ORIGIN OF THE SPIRITUAL WORLD

the formation of water, angels, the shaping or cutting out of stars out of fire, the positioning of celestial bodies at specific distances, etc. In the prophetic (or Biblical) version of my book on the formation of the universe, I addressed the processes apostrophized in the Bible. However, I could not address many of them in that book, but in this one because many believers are still skeptical. Yet, God wants us to read the Book of Enoch so we can know that He is the creator of all things and understand how there is no other God than Him. The creation narrative in the Slavonic Book of Enoch alludes to the breaking of the precursors of matter in the early universe. That book mentioned that light was above everything while darkness was below everything. "Adoil" is said to be the product of the creation of physical things from nothing, "ex nihilo", whereas "Archas" is said to have been the formation of new things from the preexisting material of "Adoil". Between the darkness below and the light above was the space in which all things were created and formed. This suggests that the universe is not infinite but limited, which is contrary to what most scientists think. Therefore, the position of the original material at the very beginning of the universe should be different from the materials in the current universe, for the whole universe is moving. According to the Book of Enoch, the first matter descended from its initial position following a command from God asking it to go down.

The Books of Enoch also detailed the formation of angels including Satan. After elucidating the formation of life on Earth, the Books of Enoch also elaborated on the corruption of the Earth by fallen angels. Like the Bible says, fallen angels and some women on Earth mated, creating the Nephilim which filled the earth with violence and abominations, which later caused God to destroy the world through the Great Flood during the time of Noah. Beside the Books of Enoch, the Book of Genesis written by Moses described how the world was corrupted by fallen angels and the giant offspring they begot after sleeping with women. The Nephilim are well described in the Bible and the Books of Enoch. I first learned about the existence of the Book of Enoch when I was listening to a speaker talking about the Nephilim.

The narrative revealed that God commissioned Enoch to publish what he saw in heaven and the Books of Enoch were supposed to be transmitted throughout generations. In other words, God did not intend for the Books of Enoch to be kept secret. Unfortunately, not only have these books been rejected by many people, but those who discovered them hid them. One thing I have come to know is that, just as God cannot be hidden, the truth about the world He created will not be rejected or hidden forever. God wished for creation to be understood by the world. Enoch prophesied that his books will be given to wise people in the last days. Thanks to the Books of Enoch, I understood that spiritual beings do not need physical food or earthly enjoyment. The pseudepigrapha also revealed that time and eternity were created by God. Details were given about the end of the world and the

CHAPTER 12: CONCLUSION

timeline of key events. By the beginning of eternity, Enoch revealed that time will be destroyed as well as all mortal things, confirming the biblical account of the End Time. For instance, Apostle Paul and Peter in the Bible also mentioned that the world will end one day and that God will destroy the world with fire. Apostle John in the Book of Revelation (Apocalypse) also had a vision of the end time and the collapse of the world. According to the Books of Enoch, Enoch taught heavenly secrets to Moses at Mount Sinai. Let's not forget that when God gave the Ten Commandment to Moses, he spent 40 days and nights on the mountain. The Books of Enoch disclosed that it was during that period that Enoch taught Moses deep secrets about creation. This may explain why the creation narrative in the Books of Enoch and the Biblical account of creation narrated by Moses in Genesis correlate a lot. When Enoch revealed these secrets to Moses, some of the angels were enraged against him. Despite him explaining to them that he did so because God gave him permission and authority, some angels did not stop arguing. God intervened and rebuked those angels, for Enoch was special in the sight of God. Indeed, among all the people who lived on Earth, Enoch is among the handful that God took to heaven alive. The account revealed how God removed Enoch, a tribute from His world under all the heavens, from humankind to be a witness against the generation of Cain on the Day of Judgment.

Enoch is also the author of the Book of Adam and others. In fact, the story said that God commanded Enoch to write the Books of Adam and Eve, he wrote that pseudepigrapha under the guidance of Archangel Michael. Those books (which I also read) gave me a deep insight into the life of Adam, Eve, and their children. The Books of Adam and Eve shed light on the life of Adam and Eve before and after their fall. For instance, Adam was able to clearly communicate with angels and was in direct contact with heaven. Those books deeply counted the fall of humankind and its immediate consequence. For instance, the eyes of Adam and Eve changed after they sinned, the spectrum of their eyes was reduced and they could not see clearly in the spiritual as they used to. Although some people think that the forbidden fruit was the best one in the Garden of Eden, the Books of Adam and Even said the opposite, for they were other fruits better than it, implying that Adam and Eve disobeyed God not because they lacked fruits. The pains inflicted by God should wake people up and cause them to seek Him. Unfortunately, that is not usually the case as most people prefer disobeying God, while dwelling temporarily in their sins, not knowing that they are setting themselves for eternal punishments.

Before the fall, wild animals were obedient to Adam and Eve, and Adam had a bright nature and could see to heaven. In the Garden of Eden, Adam and Eve could see the angels praising God in heaven, but after they sinned, that ability was lost. Many things they could easily see before their sin became hidden to them afterwards. Before Adam and Eve fell, cherubs used to

ORIGIN OF THE SPIRITUAL WORLD

tremble before them but afterward, the reverse happened. Before Adam and Eve fell, fire could not burn, but afterward, fire scorched them. Before the fall, the snake used to be the most beautiful animal, but after it became the least and the meanest of all animals. In other words, the snake was changed after God cursed it following the rebellion of Lucifer. For instance, of all the main animals in the bush, snakes are the only one that does not make a clear sound. God muted the snake after it continued attaching Adam and Eve, and even tried to kill them after their fall. The Book of Jubilees also revealed that, on the day that God punished the snake, Adam, and Eve, He removed speech from all animals for they used to communicate with Adam and Eve before. Likewise, human beings lost their original covering after they sinned. Hence, since the beginning of human clothing, clothes that humans wear is a sign of weakness and of death that humans put on, prophetically reminding them of the token of death on their bodies.

When they were in paradise in the Garden, Adam and Eve did not know the many blessings and privileges they had. They took them for granted until they were removed after they sinned. Likewise, many people today ignore their privileges and the grace of God. Some acknowledge the blessings they had only after they lose them and regrets sink in. Some people are even refusing to believe in God today, not knowing that a time is coming when they will look back and regret that decision of unbelief, but unfortunately it will be too late. The Books of Adam and Eve show that the reason Satan always attacked Adam and Eve and even most human beings today is that he sought to destroy them and overtake the Earth so he could rule it together with demons. God did not give Satan power over Adam, but Adam fell under the rule of Satan by accepting Satan's counsel. In other words, unlike what some people think, Satan did not receive the rulership of this world from God. But it was Adam who gave it away by choosing to obey Satan's command.

As you end this book, I would ask you to reflect on its content with an open mind and also get a copy of the other books I wrote about the origin of the universe. Even if some of the things I addressed here may seem strange to you, they are worth knowing. If those who compiled the Bible did not reject the pseudepigraphic books I discussed here, they would be in the Bible today. In fact, until today, some churches have some of those books in their Bible. For instance, many of the rejected books still exist in some catholic and orthodox Bibles. Therefore, I urge you not to deny all of the mysteries I decoded and recounted in this book, for (despite human errors in their transmitting them throughout the generations) all of them are Scriptures inspired by God, and denying them may equal how some unbelievers refuse the word of God in the Bible thinking that the Bible is not inspired by God or that there is no God. For indeed, there is a God who created everything and who revealed many things to our ancestors, but some of them refused to

CHAPTER 12: CONCLUSION

listen. Let us not make the same mistake.

I wrote many other books and if you would like to learn about them, please visit www.Science180.com. If you want to talk to me, work with me, partner with me, or donate to help me take this message to the world, please visit my personal website: www.Israel120.com.

NEXT STEPS OF THE JOURNEY

Get free resources on Science180.com
If you have finished reading this book and would like to learn more about my discoveries and how they can help you, you are at the right place. Indeed, I am really committed to helping you address any questions that you may still have concerning the origin, functioning, and fate of the universe, and how you can partner or collaborate with me for greater results.

To get free resources that will help you understand other aspects of the universe formation not covered in this book, visit Science180.com and my personal website Israel120.com. On those sites, I will be sharing guides and strategies to get the most out of my initiatives. I will also be sharing my favorite references, tips, next-steps readings and other important things in the pipeline that will help you regardless of your field of expertise, interest, and needs.

Subscribe to "Science180 Newsletter": The only accurate universe-origin, life-origin, and chemicals-origin newsletter in the whole world!
Be a part of decoding the universe-origin, life-origin, and chemicals-origin! Get origin-related news, information, discoveries, updates, announcements, news, reviews, articles, educational materials, and opportunities, from a holistic perspective not available anywhere else so you can participate in and enjoy decoding the origin, current state, and fate of the universe and its content. You will also receive priceless tips about how Nathanael-Israel thinks, what are his secrets and initiatives, what he has accomplished, and what he recommends. Without any delay, sign up for Science180 Newsletter today at Science180.com/newsletter. It is free!

Speaking engagement
Since the beginning of humanity, only Nathanael-Israel Israel, and nobody else, has offered a scientific explanation of the formation of the universe that perfectly matches science and the Biblical account of creation.

Unlike all other creationist speakers, Nathanael-Israel Israel known as the first person in the whole world that calculated the mathematical equations that scientifically demonstrated that the Earth was formed 2.82 days after the beginning of the universe, while the Moon and the Sun were formed 3.32 days and 3.69 days respectively after the beginning of the universe, therefore confirming the 3500 years old Biblical account of creation according to which the formation of the Earth was completed on the 3rd day, according to which the Moon and the Sun were completed on the 4th day of creation.

Nathanael-Israel Israel is also the first person in history to scientifically demonstrate that each day in the Biblical account of creation was literally 24 hours, a milestone that accurately reconciled science and the Bible, and that overturned the myth according to which some people have thought that each day of creation was millions of years (a misunderstanding that caused many people to deny God, the Creator). Therefore, Nathanael-Israel Israel ushered a new era for the proper understanding of the Biblical account of creation and its application to decode the universe and its content for the benefits of humankind. He has provided an undeniable reconciliation of science and the Biblical account of creation. He is known as the one who offered the most accurate explanation of the Biblical account of creation.

When you hire Nathanael-Israel Israel, you will learn from the historic specialist of universe-origin questions what is the proven formula that demonstrates the formation of the Earth on the 3rd day of creation, and the formation of the Moon and Sun on the 4th day.

To book Dr. Nathanael-Israel Israel for a speaking engagement purpose, visit Science180.com/speaking.

In addition to writing groundbreaking books and engaging in other business endeavors, Nathanael-Israel Israel is a renowned speaker, who you can invite to speak at your organization.

Values that Dr. Nathanael-Israel Israel can add to your life include:
- Rare expertise and tips that will increase your abilities
- Usefulness that will advance your impact regardless of your field of expertise
- Understanding of the world that will sharpen your perspective
- Critical information that will positively change your life
- Experiences turned into insight that will motivate and guide you
- Irrefutable scientific proofs of the existence of God that will save you time and launch you into a zone of unlimited opportunities
- Unquestionable scientific proofs of how God created the universe
- Accurate demonstration of the historic formula that reconciled science and the Bible
- Enlightenment that will help people to start using their brain instead of just praying and expecting God to do everything for them

For speaking inquiries, including how you can get Dr. Nathanael-Israel Israel to speak to your organization or at an event, visit Science180.com/speaking for more details.

As the standout scientific authority who accurately decoded the universe, Nathanael-Israel Israel has been helping countless people across the globe to discover and understand the complex origin of the universe without leaving

NEXT STEPS OF THE JOURNEY

out the challenging questions that people of all ages have been struggling to answer for thousands of years! As the true go-to expert when it comes to the formation of the universe and of life, Nathanael-Israel believes that, regardless of age, background, culture, religion, profession, everyone deserves to understand how the universe and life were formed and how they can leverage on that knowledge to improve lives nonstop. Therefore, his groundbreaking discoveries of the formation of the universe, life, and chemicals have been broken down into books tailored to scientists (including physicists, chemists, biologists, mathematicians), laypeople or general public, believers and freethinkers, philosophers, children, etc., therefore maximizing the benefits to humanity. These historic, internationally-acclaimed origin books include:

- "Turbulent Origin of the Universe"
- "Reconciling Science and Creation Accurately"
- "Turbulent Origin of Chemical Particles"
- "From Science to Bible's Conclusions"
- "Turbulent Origin of Life"
- "Origin of the Spiritual World"
- "How Baby Universe Was Born"
- "How God Created Baby Universe"
- "Science180 Accurate Scientific Proof of God"

When you hire Nathanael-Israel Israel to speak at your organization, you will:

- scientifically learn how the Earth was formed on the 3rd day of creation
- logically learn how the Sun and the Moon were formed on the 4th day of creation
- get specific in-depth knowledge, up-to-the-minute information, ideas, and insights about the universe-origin, life-origin, and chemicals-origin so that you expand your market, cut useless costs, stop wasting time on inadequate projects, and start focusing on the profitable solutions
- get relevant universe-origin stories that are specific to your field of expertise
- learn from a cooperative, flexible, and an easy to work with expert who will respond to your universe formation needs and position you to stay on top of your competitors
- interact with a renowned expert that will not just lecture you, but that will help you sort out your origin-related questions using strategies to tap into deep secrets you ignore

- listen to an experienced expert who discovered outstanding secrets about the origin of all there is
- learn authentic information not from someone who just reads you a PowerPoint, but from the true go-to expert (when it comes to critical cosmological problems) who will share with you both his mistakes and successes that will help you get much closer to the better life you want to live
- revolutionize every origin-related domain with your accurate understanding of the universe-origin
- hear Dr. Nathanael-Israel Israel's personal selection and teaching of key topics that will help you break the code of the universe formation and functioning, and strategically enlighten you, guide you to navigate and filter the massive data collected on the universe and its content so you know how to answer the world's most challenging origin questions, remove any scientific and philosophical cataracts that may be blocking you, and help bring you many steps closer to your best life today and forever
- hear the greatest scientific and philosophic lessons of some top scientists, philosophers, thinkers, and public figures who have realized historic mistakes they made in life (concerning the origin of the universe, life, and chemicals), and that they corrected thanks to the discoveries of Nathanael-Israel Israel, who founded Science180, and who is acknowledged as the scientist that truly decrypted the universe-origin for the first time
- Get world key lessons successful people have learned in life and how people can learn from their experiences to improve lives instead of repeating their mistakes that many people still ignore at their own perils

To book Dr. Nathanael-Israel Israel for a speaking engagement purpose, visit Science180.com/speaking.

How you can make money by joining the affiliate program to sell Nathanael-Israel Israel's books

Greetings,

Do you want to make easy money by selling the #1 universe-origin, life-origin, and chemicals-origin books on your website, newsletter, and by mail? You can start making big money as you help sell Science180 Books including this one on your website and network. Indeed, by now, you know that I operate a website called Science180.com, specialized in helping people across the globe to scientifically decode and understand the formation of the universe, life, and chemicals.

Your contacts, site, blog, forum, podcast, and newsletter may be admired among my target audience. Some of my products and services may be of interest to your audience. My books are the first in history to scientifically demonstrate the match between science and Biblical creation in a way that satisfies both believers and nonbelievers, a historic achievement and discovery that is revolutionizing our view of the origin of the universe, life, and chemicals for the benefit of humankind.

Imagine you have a website where you can talk to people about my books and services and get a great percentage of every purchase they do on my site? Imagine you send a certain link about my books to your friends or network and, when any of your contacts buy a copy of my books, you get a percentage or a certain amount of what they pay on my sites. Imagine you can email your friends and spread the good news about my books and when anyone uses that link to buy my books, I give you something. Well! This is what the affiliate program is about. Apply today or learn more about it at Science180.com/affiliate. Likewise, if you own a website, you can apply for Science180's affiliate program, and I will send you a specific affiliate link that you will place on your website and newsletter, and if people click on it to buy my books, they will be led to my page and after they buy, I will pay you a certain amount, sharing the profit with you instead of just verbally saying thank you.

Would you be interested in reviewing some of my products and services with the aim of becoming an affiliate? We have a wonderful affiliate program and commissions are paid quickly and accurately.

If you are satisfied by the quality of our products and services, I am convinced you will also be impressed by our affiliate program.

I look forward to hearing from you

Nathanael-Israel Israel, PhD

Collaborate or partner with Nathanael-Israel Israel

If you have any lawful idea, initiative, or suggestion for a genuine partnership with Dr. Nathanael-Israel Israel or Science180, please visit Science180.com/partner to inform us.

How to be trained or mentored by or have a one-on-one consulting with Dr. Nathanael-Israel Israel

Hire Nathanael-Israel Israel to train you or your organization in the best ways to conduct yourself and your organization to align your initiatives with the real understanding of the origin of the universe, of life, and of chemical particles in a way that you will not hear anywhere else. Nathanael-Israel Israel offers training through the program called "Science180 Academy". For training purposes, please visit Science180Academy.com.

Visit Nathanael-Israel Israel's personal website to get for free great resources you won't find anywhere else

To stay in touch with, Dr. Nathanael-Israel Israel, and to get updates directly from him, please visit his website, Israel120.com, and sign up for his popular newsletter at Israel120.com/newsletter for free.

Ask for review

If you are a book reviewer or a professional wanting to review this book or others written by Nathanael-Israel Israel, please contact us at Science180.com/AskForReview

Donate and support Nathanael-Israel Israel's efforts and initiatives

To help humankind accurately understand the real origin of the universe and its content, like I have done in the groundbreaking books I published after 12 years of sacrifice, I need your financial support. Please consider donating to me or to Science180 by visiting Israel120.com/donate or Science180.com/donate.

Your donation will be used to help me continue doing what I did to birth these books that you enjoyed and that you know will help many people across globe. No amount of money is too small or too big. Whatever you can give, please give.

Quantity discounts: Purchase Science180 books including this one in bulk at a special discount

To purchase Science180 books including this one in bulk at a special discount for sales promotion, corporate gifts, fund-raising, or educational purposes or to create special editions to specifications, contact specialsales@science180.com or visit Science180.com/discount.

Buy a copy of Nathanael-Israel Israel's books for your friends, family, or someone

If this book has been a blessing to you, and we know it has, please consider getting another copy and giving it to a friend, a family member, or someone you think it may help or challenge. If you want to get many copies, we can even give you a discount; just contact us as we previously explained.

Recommend Nathanael-Israel Israel's books to your organization

Because I know this book has been a blessing to you, I ask that you recommend it and others that I wrote to your organization, class, workplace, church, school, network, or clubs. Recommending this book will help others

NEXT STEPS OF THE JOURNEY

to tap into the blessing and opportunities that my books will open for them.

Share Nathanael-Israel Israel's groundbreaking discovery with others

To improve more lives, please share the findings of Nathanael-Israel Israel's books with others, for many people out there still do not understand how the universe was formed and sharing your experience of reading this book will help them. If you enjoy Nathanael-Israel Israel's books, please help other people find them by writing a book review on your blog or on online bookstores, or write it and share it with us. Likewise, share and mention this book on your social media platforms (e.g. Facebook, Twitter, YouTube, etc.).

Follow Nathanael-Israel Israel on social media

In our modern world, social medias have become a huge part of how messages spread across the globe today. To ensure more people hear about the good news revealed in my books, I need you to follow me and share my contents on your social medias and in your network. To know the full list of my social media accounts and follow me please visit Science180.com/socialmedia.

Share your feedback, critics, testimony, experience, adventures, story, or comment about this book with me

How has Nathanael-Israel Israel's books and services at Science180 improved your life? I would love to hear from you.

To help me know how I can better help you next and encourage others, I need to know and capture your testimony or critics. Please visit the feedback page, science180.com/feedback, to tell me:

- how this book impacted you or will impact you
- what you like or dislike or disagree with
- what you think, wish, or dream that I need to work on next
- what you wish to see in this book but that was absent
- what shocked you the most
- what got your heart pumping as you were reading this book
- what you found more insightful or thought-provoking
- what you want to do to be a part of my journey
- how my work changed your life or someone else's life

Message from the publisher of this book

Just like Nathanael-Israel Israel, you can publish your book(s) with us too. To get started and see how we may help you, please visit Science180Publishing.com today.

To contact Nathanael-Israel Israel or Science180

For any suggestions or questions, please visit Science180.com/contact and Nathanael-Israel Israel's personal website: Israel120.com. Feel free to ask me any questions you have about the universe formation, life formation, and chemicals formation.

INDEX

REFERENCES

Lumpkin B. Joseph (2010). The encyclopedia of lost and rejected scriptures: The pseudepigrapha and apocrypha. Fifth Estate. Alabama, USA. 825 pages.

Israel Nathanael-Israel (2025a). Turbulent Origin of the Universe. Science180, Augusta, USA 683 pages.

Israel Nathanael-Israel (2025b). From Science to Bible's Conclusions. Science180, Augusta, USA 170 pages.

Israel Nathanael-Israel (2025c). Reconciling Science and Creation Accurately. Science180, Augusta, USA 299 pages.

Israel Nathanael-Israel (2025d). Turbulent Origin of Chemical Particles. Science180, Augusta, USA 397 pages.

Israel Nathanael-Israel (2025e). Turbulent Origin of Life. Science180, Augusta, USA 370 pages.

Israel Nathanael-Israel (2025f). Origin of the Spiritual World. Science180, Augusta, USA 151 pages.

Israel Nathanael-Israel (2025g). How Baby Universe Was Born. Science180, Augusta, USA 130 pages.

Israel Nathanael-Israel (2025h). How God Created Baby Universe. Science180, Augusta, USA 224 pages.

Israel Nathanael-Israel (2025i). Science180 Accurate Scientific Proof of God. Science180, Augusta, USA 214 pages.

ORIGIN OF THE SPIRITUAL WORLD

INDEX

INDEX

A

Abraham 4
Abyss 35, 39, 68, 114
Adam and Eve 3, 4, 18, 29, 43, 63, 64, 65, 68, 69, 71, 72, 73, 74, 77, 78, 79, 80, 82, 83, 84, 85, 86, 87, 88, 89, 90, 91, 94, 101, 102, 103, 104, 105, 120, 121, 123, 128, 131, 132
Adoil 30, 31, 32, 33, 34, 129, 130
Africa 2, 6, 105
African 6
After the fall 90, 121
Albert Einstein 3, 14
American 5, 150
Anak 97
Ancient scriptures 8, 150
Angels... 1, 2, 6, 7, 11, 12, 13, 14, 15, 18, 20, 21, 23, 29, 42, 45, 46, 47, 48, 49, 52, 53, 54, 55, 56, 58, 59, 63, 64, 65, 68, 69, 71, 72, 73, 74, 80, 82, 83, 84, 85, 86, 87, 89, 90, 94, 95, 96, 97, 104, 105, 111, 114, 119, 121, 122, 124, 125, 126, 128, 129, 130, 131
Animal speech 73, 74
Apocalypse 90, 110, 126, 131
Apocrypha 4
ARABOTH RAQIA 50
Archangel 24, 25, 68, 120
Archas 33, 34, 35, 129, 130
Arkhas 33
Asteroids 2, 23, 39, 129

B

Baby Universe 143
Before the fall of Man ... 63, 73, 131, 132
Beginning 8, 9, 11, 21, 22, 29, 31, 41, 54, 63, 64, 72, 77, 79, 80, 83, 85, 86, 87, 101, 106, 109, 110, 111, 112, 113, 121, 122, 130, 131, 132, 135, 151
Belly 30, 31, 34, 73, 74, 129
Beninese 151
Bible 2, 6, 1, 3, 4, 7, 8, 29, 31, 32, 33, 40, 41, 42, 43, 47, 49, 63, 71, 74, 77, 78, 80, 88, 94, 96, 97, 110, 113, 114, 120, 121, 122, 126, 128, 129, 130, 131, 132, 136, 137, 143, 150, 151
Biblical 2, 6, 3, 4, 9, 25, 28, 32, 36, 41, 68, 126, 130, 131, 135, 136, 139, 150
Biblical account of creation 9
Big Bang 2, 150
Billions of years 150
Book of Adam and Eve 64, 73, 77, 78, 79, 80, 83, 84, 85, 87, 89, 90, 102, 103, 104, 106, 120
Book of Jasher 3, 113, 128
Book of Jubilees 4, 40, 45, 63, 68, 89, 90, 128, 132
Book of the Palaces 6
Books of Enoch 6, 3, 4, 5, 6, 7, 8, 11, 15, 19, 23, 25, 28, 31, 40, 41, 43, 49, 63, 68, 89, 90, 95, 96, 113, 120, 123, 128, 129, 130
Burst asunder 30

C

Cain 14, 126, 131
Calendar 22, 111, 112
Celestial bodies . 5, 7, 12, 13, 15, 16, 21, 22, 23, 32, 34, 36, 37, 39, 40, 43, 45, 46, 47, 111, 112, 129, 130
Chaos 39, 46
Chayoth 20, 47, 52, 53, 55, 57
CHAYYLIEL 47, 52

145

Science180: Understand the Creation of the Universe. Increase Your Glory and Peace of Mind

Chemical particles 36, 139
Chemical reactions 21
Cherubim . 12, 18, 19, 20, 24, 46, 47, 53, 54, 55, 57, 126
Christianity 7
Church of His Presence 96
Circuit of 28 years 22
Circuit of 532 years 22
collapse of the universe 110, 113, 114, 131
Commandments .. 25, 41, 77, 78, 84, 89, 91, 96
Constellations 24, 42, 47, 48, 95
Corruption 65, 94, 95, 96, 130
Cosmology 2, 3, 4, 5, 6, 7, 14, 15, 16, 138
Creation 6, 2, 3, 4, 5, 8, 9, 11, 13, 14, 16, 22, 23, 25, 28, 29, 30, 31, 32, 33, 35, 36, 39, 40, 41, 45, 49, 59, 69, 72, 74, 79, 80, 89, 110, 112, 113, 119, 120, 122, 124, 125, 127, 128, 130, 131, 135, 136, 137, 139, 143, 150
Creator 2, 6, 7, 53, 56, 111, 136
Creatures .. 40, 42, 43, 54, 65, 69, 72, 74, 85, 86, 89, 90, 91, 97, 102, 109, 113

D

Darkness .. 33, 34, 35, 36, 42, 45, 55, 64, 72, 79, 84, 85, 110, 111, 125, 130
Days of creation 150
Death ... 2, 42, 52, 72, 73, 80, 83, 85, 86, 96, 102, 103, 104, 110, 125, 132
Demons 1, 2, 85, 94, 97, 98, 101, 122, 132
Disobedience 89, 96
Doubts 2

E

Earth 1, 2, 8, 9, 11, 12, 13, 16, 17, 28, 29, 31, 35, 36, 37, 38, 39, 42, 43, 47, 65, 68, 69, 77, 86, 94, 102, 103, 104, 106, 110, 112, 113, 114, 120, 121, 122, 123, 124, 125, 126, 129, 130, 131, 132, 135, 136, 137
Earthquake 19, 47, 114
End time 110, 114, 131
Enoch 3, 4, 5, 6, 7, 11, 12, 13, 14, 15, 16, 17, 18, 19, 20, 21, 22, 23, 24, 25, 28, 29, 30, 31, 33, 34, 35, 36, 38, 39, 40, 42, 43, 46, 47, 48, 49, 52, 53, 54, 55, 56, 57, 58, 63, 65, 68, 69, 89, 90, 91, 94, 95, 96, 109, 110, 111, 112, 113, 114, 119, 120, 121, 122, 123, 124, 125, 126, 128, 129, 130, 131
Essenes 7
Eternity . 6, 24, 25, 41, 109, 110, 113, 130, 131
Ethiopic Book of Enoch 5, 15
Ezekiel 55, 69

F

Fall of Adam .. 18, 29, 69, 77, 78, 89, 91, 121
Fall of Satan 68, 71
FIFTH HEAVEN 50
Fire 12, 21, 24, 40, 41, 43, 45, 46, 47, 51, 52, 53, 54, 55, 57, 59, 64, 78, 79, 80, 83, 84, 85, 102, 103, 110, 121, 123, 129, 130, 131, 132
Firmament 16, 24, 39, 45, 49
FIRST HEAVEN 49
Foundation of the universe .. 30, 31, 33, 129
Foundations of the universe . 16, 29, 40, 43, 53, 113
FOURTH HEAVEN 49
Fragmentation 31, 129
Fruit of knowledge 78

INDEX

G

Gabriel.....24, 28, 29, 46, 47, 48, 104
GALGALLIEL..................................48
Garden of Eden ... 18, 20, 43, 63, 64, 69, 77, 80, 84, 85, 88, 89, 90, 101, 102, 103, 104, 121, 123, 131
Genesis.....4, 5, 6, 18, 25, 28, 35, 40, 41, 42, 49, 55, 69, 74, 78, 90, 94, 95, 96, 97, 122, 130, 131, 150
Gnosticism.....................................33
God..... 2, 6, 2, 3, 4, 5, 6, 7, 8, 11, 12, 14, 18, 19, 20, 22, 23, 24, 25, 28, 29, 30, 31, 32, 33, 34, 35, 36, 38, 39, 40, 41, 42, 43, 45, 46, 47, 49, 54, 55, 59, 63, 64, 65, 68, 69, 71, 72, 73, 74, 77, 78, 79, 80, 82, 83, 84, 85, 86, 87, 89, 90, 91, 94, 95, 96, 97, 101, 102, 103, 104, 105, 109, 110, 111, 112, 113, 114, 119, 120, 121, 122, 123, 124, 125, 126, 128, 129, 130, 131, 132, 136, 137, 150, 151
Gravity..43
Great circuit 22
Gregorian calendar 112

H

Heaven .6, 11, 12, 13, 14, 16, 17, 20, 21, 22, 23, 24, 25, 29, 31, 32, 33, 35, 39, 40, 41, 43, 45, 46, 47, 48, 49, 50, 51, 52, 53, 54, 55, 56, 57, 58, 59, 63, 65, 69, 71, 72, 74, 78, 82, 83, 84, 85, 94, 95, 96, 97, 103, 105, 111, 112, 113, 114, 119, 120, 121, 123, 124, 125, 126, 128, 129, 130, 131
Hebrew Book of Enoch... 6, 122, 124
Hidden books 4, 5
Highest things 30, 32, 33

I

Immortal 32, 124
Incorruptible 32, 124
Invisible 2, 15, 29, 30, 33, 43, 47, 129
Irin and Qaddishin 48, 55, 58, 59
Isaac Newton...................................3
Isaiah 43
Israel.......2, 4, 3, 8, 9, 51, 54, 57, 97, 111, 113, 123, 135, 136, 137, 138, 139, 140, 141, 142, 143, 150

J

Jesus Christ.... 5, 6, 29, 47, 102, 103, 104, 113, 123, 125
Jewish 3, 7, 36, 89, 105, 112
Jews 3, 5, 6, 89, 97, 102, 112, 120
John Kilpatrick 96
Joshua............................3, 112, 123
Jude 5, 96
Judeo-Christian..............................7
Judge animals 65, 91
Judgment..... 21, 41, 57, 58, 96, 109, 126, 131
Judgment day 95, 96

K

KERUBIEL 47, 53
KOKBIEL..48

L

Largest star in the universe 23
Last days.......................................65
Life....2, 3, 4, 8, 9, 11, 12, 20, 28, 29, 42, 43, 45, 51, 52, 55, 63, 64, 77, 83, 90, 91, 94, 101, 103, 110, 111, 120, 123, 125, 128, 130, 131, 135, 136, 137, 138, 139, 141, 142, 150, 151
Light... 12, 14, 16, 19, 21, 23, 24, 25, 30, 31, 32, 33, 34, 35, 36, 42, 45, 46, 47, 53, 56, 57, 58, 63, 64, 68, 77, 79, 80, 84, 85, 104, 110, 111, 112, 114, 120, 123, 125, 129, 130, 131
Lord ... 11, 12, 19, 20, 21, 23, 24, 28, 29, 40, 41, 43, 45, 64, 65, 77, 91,

102, 103, 109, 110, 114, 120, 121, 122, 124, 125
Lord's prayer 102, 103
Lowest things 34, 129

M

Marzulli 96
Mathematics 9, 135
Messiah 5, 7, 41
Metatron 6, 122, 124
Methuselah 11, 12, 114, 124, 126
Michael .24, 25, 46, 48, 72, 120, 131
Milky Way Galaxy 15
Moon 8, 9, 12, 14, 15, 16, 22, 23, 28, 42, 47, 48, 57, 74, 95, 112, 113, 114, 129, 135, 136, 137
Moses 4, 6, 35, 45, 69, 90, 95, 96, 97, 111, 112, 121, 122, 130, 131
Motion of celestial bodies 22
Mount Hermon 94
Movement of the Sun 15, 16

N

Nakedness 80, 110
Nathanael-Israel Israel 2, 4, 8, 9, 135, 136, 137, 138, 139, 140, 141, 142, 143, 150
Nephilim 96, 97, 98, 130
New Testament 5, 96
Noah .5, 6, 14, 39, 97, 105, 122, 130
Non-being 29
Non-existent 29
North Pole 6, 31

O

Obedience 65
Old Testament 7
OPHANNIEL 48
Ophannim 21, 48, 55, 56, 57, 126
OPHPHANNIEL 48, 56
Origin of Chemical Particles 143
Origin of Life 143

P

Paradise 63, 69, 84, 89, 96, 110, 111, 132
Paul 41, 110, 131
Peter 41, 110, 131
Physical things 2, 29, 30, 35, 46, 130
Physical world 2, 28, 30, 31, 129
Plants 2, 42, 43, 91, 95
Pravuil 25
Precursor of the physical world ... 30
Precursors 30, 31, 32, 34, 35, 36, 39, 40, 110, 129, 130
Preexisting materials 33
Prison 95, 96
Prophets 6, 41, 69, 120, 123
Pseudepigrapha 4, 5, 28, 68, 90, 120, 130, 131, 143
Pseudepigraphic .. 6, 3, 8, 31, 36, 77, 89, 109, 132

R

RADWERIEL 48, 57
Raguel 46
RAHATIEL 48
Raphael 46, 95, 104
Raqa 49
Rejected scriptures 5
Religion 4
Remiel 46
Resurrection 102
Revelation ... 6, 72, 74, 96, 110, 113, 114, 126, 131
Righteousness 41, 58, 124, 126
RIKBIEL 47, 52
Rocks 18, 39, 46, 102

S

Sabbath 89
Salvation 31, 41, 101, 102, 103
Saraqael 46
Satan 1, 19, 55, 57, 68, 69, 71, 72, 73, 74, 78, 79, 83, 84, 85, 89, 91,

INDEX

94, 101, 102, 104, 130, 132
Science ... 2, 6, 3, 8, 9, 15, 25, 32, 36, 40, 137, 150, 151
Science180 ..... 2, 3, 4, 8, 40, 41, 126, 133, 135, 136, 137, 138, 139, 140, 141, 142, 151
Science180 Academy 139, 151
Second Book of Enoch 5
SECOND HEAVEN 49
Secrets 1, 2, 3, 5, 8, 11, 23, 25, 28, 29, 57, 95, 96, 112, 114, 119, 120, 121, 122, 123, 128, 131, 135, 137, 138
Semyaza 94, 95
SERAPHIEL 48, 56, 57
Seraphim 24, 48, 55, 56, 57, 126
SEVENTH HEAVEN 50
SHAHAQIEL 48
SHEKINA 50
Sin 29, 43, 63, 64, 65, 79, 80, 82, 83, 84, 85, 86, 87, 89, 90, 114, 131, 132
Sins .57, 72, 73, 79, 83, 87, 103, 109, 121, 131
SIXTH HEAVEN 50
Sky .. 2, 15, 16, 36, 40, 49, 56, 58, 97, 111
Slavonic Secrets of Enoch 6
Snake 73, 74, 132
Solar System 14, 15, 23
Space .. 12, 13, 14, 15, 23, 30, 34, 35, 49, 52, 128, 130
Spirits 1, 2, 45, 46, 54, 95, 96
Spiritual 1, 2, 3, 4, 7, 8, 12, 14, 15, 18, 21, 28, 29, 30, 33, 40, 42, 43, 46, 47, 54, 82, 85, 89, 95, 110, 119, 125, 129, 130, 131
Spiritual World 143
Stars 2, 12, 14, 15, 16, 21, 23, 35, 36, 37, 40, 42, 43, 48, 55, 56, 57, 96, 110, 111, 114, 128, 129, 130

Sun 8, 9, 12, 14, 15, 16, 21, 22, 23, 28, 29, 35, 36, 40, 41, 46, 48, 56, 85, 110, 112, 128, 129, 135, 136, 137
Supernatural 3, 21, 25

T

Tanakh 7
Third Book of Enoch 6
THIRD HEAVEN 49
Throne of God . 6, 12, 14, 18, 21, 24, 30, 31, 32, 34, 52, 68, 95, 113, 114, 119, 123, 129

U

UFO 5, 96
Universe 6, 1, 2, 3, 4, 5, 6, 7, 8, 9, 11, 12, 13, 14, 15, 16, 18, 21, 22, 23, 25, 28, 29, 30, 31, 32, 34, 35, 36, 41, 43, 46, 47, 48, 49, 52, 54, 55, 56, 57, 59, 94, 109, 113, 114, 123, 128, 129, 130, 132, 135, 136, 137, 138, 139, 140, 141, 142, 150, 151
Uriel 22, 46
USA 143

V

Visible 15, 29, 30, 33, 43, 54, 129

W

Watchers and Holy Ones 48, 58
Water .. 6, 14, 19, 35, 36, 37, 39, 40, 41, 43, 45, 46, 49, 64, 73, 87, 104, 129, 130
Wednesday 42
Winds 12, 14, 15, 16, 17, 18, 19, 20, 21, 23, 47, 52, 57, 129
Wobbling of the Sun 16

ABOUT THE AUTHOR

You have heard people say that God created the universe in 6 days, while others claimed that the Big Bang did it instead through billions of years processes, but until now, you have never heard of a human being that mathematically demonstrated the Biblical account of creation accurately using the great scientific raw data hidden in wrong scientific theories and in ancient scriptures that were hidden or rejected. Indeed, after focusing on scientifically cracking some of the world's most unsolved problems, Dr. Nathanael-Israel Israel discovered that, the reason most believers have not scientifically understood the creation of the universe is that they have spent years reading the Genesis story (but neglected to properly ponder on ancient revelations about the origin of the universe and life), while they learned nearly nothing about how to properly interpret it using the scientific data without checking neither their faith nor their mind at the door. The result of this attitude is that most believers learned to study and memorize all kinds of biblical verses and metaphorical interpretations of creation, while they trash secular theories with all their amazing raw data, but they never learned how to unconventionally acknowledge the fact that the biblical account of creation is a literal and chronological history that they are struggling to rationally decode, but that can be explained scientifically without compromise... so they can have key ancient revelations and scientific raw data (denuded of the theories wrapping them) to properly work for and lead them to the demonstration of the conclusion of the Bible rather than starting with the accurate conclusion that, unfortunately, usually chases away rationalists and skeptics: God really created the universe in six 24-hours literal consecutive days indeed.

How can some believers abandon wrong creationist theories if they think it is impossible for science to literally prove the Genesis story, or if they think that science is evil and diametrically opposed to faith, or if they continue to compromisingly embrace scientific theories that totally contradict the Bible as if anyone can help God by alleging that the Biblical account of creation, written before the scientific era, lied or is inaccurate? How can the skeptics believe in the Biblical narrative of creation if most believers can't even properly prove it scientifically?

Lucky you, that is where Dr. Nathanael-Israel Israel came in to reanalyze the scientific raw data with an original perspective to unlock the ultimate and only solution believers and skeptics have been looking for throughout the ages... Dr. Nathanael-Israel Israel is a member of the American Chemical Society, American Association for the Advancement of Science, American Society of Agricultural and Biological Engineers, American Society for

Microbiology, American Society of Biochemistry and Molecular Biology, Ecological Society of America, American Society of Agronomy, Crop Science Society of America, and Soil Science Society of America. He is the founder of Science180, the American organization that operates Science180 Academy (Science180Academy.com), a non-degree training, speaking, consulting, and mentoring program designed to groom, and empower people of all backgrounds in the truth about the origin of the universe, life, and chemicals. Before launching Science180, Nathanael-Israel Israel worked as a scientist at a major 500 Fortune biotechnological company in the USA, where he also founded and owns a news company. Some of the groundbreaking books of this Beninese-American include:

1. Turbulent Origin of the Universe
2. Reconciling Science and Creation Accurately
3. Turbulent Origin of Chemical Particles
4. Origin of the Spiritual World
5. From Science to Bible's Conclusions
6. Turbulent Origin of Life
7. How Baby Universe Was Born
8. How God Created Baby Universe
9. Science180 Accurate Scientific Proof of God

Get these thoughtful books to figure out what happened at the beginning of the universe, what is coming up, and why it is time to urgently rethink everything you have been told about the universe-origin so you don't eventually regret! Connect with this extraordinary scientist and get some free resources today by visiting Israel120.com.

Nathanael-Israel Israel: Has had the honor to be acknowledged the First Human Being that Scientifically Reconciled Science and the Biblical Account of Creation

www.ingramcontent.com/pod-product-compliance
Lightning Source LLC
Chambersburg PA
CBHW060505030426
42337CB00015B/1754